Harold J. Westing
Penny Thome

BUILDING BIBLICAL VALUES

Innovative Learning Exercises for All Ages

kregel
RESOURCES

Grand Rapids, MI 49501

Building Biblical Values

Copyright © 1996 by Harold J. Westing and Penny Thome

Published by Kregel Resources, an imprint of Kregel Publications, P.O. Box 2607, Grand Rapids, MI 49501. Kregel
Resources provides timely and relevant resources for Christian
life and service. Your comments and suggestions are valued.

All rights reserved. No part of this book may be reproduced,
stored in a retrieval system, or transmitted in any form or
by any means—electronic, mechanical, photocopy, recording, or otherwise—without written permission of the pub-
lisher, except for brief quotations in printed reviews.

Unless otherwise indicated, all Scripture quotations are from
The Holy Bible: New International Version © 1978 by the
International Bible Society. Used by permission of
Zondervan Publishing House.

Cover design: Alan G. Hartman
Book design: Nicholas G. Richardson

Library of Congress Cataloging-in-Publication Data
Westing, Harold J.
   Building biblical values / Harold J. Westing and Penny
Thome.
        p.   cm.
   Includes bibliographical references and index.
   1. Games in Christian education. 2. Values—Study and
teaching. 3. Church work with youth. 4. Church work
with families. 5. Youth—Conduct of life. I. Thome,
Penelope L. II. Title.
BV1536.3.W48   1996   268'6—dc20   95-38815
                                                                  CIP

ISBN 0-8254-3957-4

                Printed in the United States of America
                   1 2 3 4 5 / 00 99 98 97 96

Contents

Exercises for Adults

Appendixes

Chapter One

A Discipler's Guide to Biblical Values

On a dark night a team of thieves breaks in through the back door of a shopping center. This is an unusual team of burglars, however. They move from store to store, stealing only the price tags! When they are finished gathering tags, they mix them all up, go back through the stores, and place them at random on items throughout the stores they took them from in the first place.

When the shopping center opens in the morning, customers are stunned— fur coats are $1.59 while toothpaste is $1,479.95. Bread has suddenly jumped to $159.00, but a pair of shoes is a mere $.29. One spool of thread now costs $389.95. Everyone is flabbergasted.

It's an old illustration that author Tony Campolo made famous in his book *The Success Fantasy.*[1] While it's only an illustration, it does picture vividly what Satan has done in our society. We now find it difficult to know the true value of anything in our system. Things of enduring value—love, commitment, honesty, virtue—are regarded as cheap commodities, outdated or ready to be discarded when inconvenient. The truly cheap things of life—mindless entertainment, sensual thrills, professional success, and material satisfaction— are bought at incredibly expensive social and personal cost.

This confusion over true worth and value has alarmed a number of commentators, both secular and Christian.

For many years Malcolm Muggeridge issued dire warnings over the implications of social drifts and changing values in Europe and North America, and finally he asserted that Western civilization has collapsed at last.

> Since the beginning of the Second World War, Western Society has experienced a complete abandonment of its mores, complete abandonment of its sense of good and evil. The true crisis of our time has nothing to do with monetary troubles, unemployment or nuclear weapons.[2]

William Bennett insists that we Americans must revamp our society because it has lost its moral values. In his book, *The Devaluing of America: The Fight for Our Culture and Our Children*, Bennett gives us numerous illustrations of how America is losing its values. The following are several examples.[3]

Marriages per 1,000 women
    1960 = 73.5
    1991 = 54.2

Violent crime rate, incidents per 10,000 Americans
    1960 = 16.1
    1991 = 75.8

Suicides per 100,000 youths ages 15 to 24
    1960 = 3.65
    1990 = 11.3

Divorce rate per 1,000 married women
    1960 = 9.2
    1990 = 20.9

Average daily TV viewing (hours per household)
    1960 = 5.06
    1992 = 7.04

Abortions of pregnancies
    1972 = 12.9%
    1990 = 24.6%

Children with single mothers (of total births)
    1960 = 8%
    1990 = 22%

Births to unwed mothers (of total births)
    1960 = 5.3%
    1990 = 28%

This list, of course, is by no means complete. Each day the media presents us with news reports, documentaries, and tabloid news shows highlighting more examples of the moral decline of our society. Thus, the things most commonly valued by today's depraved society become increasingly untrustworthy because society has no transcendent standards by which to judge their worth.

In a sense, we are like the factory workers of years past who listened for the noon whistle to signal lunch break. When the whistle blew, they would then set their own watches to 12:00 noon. But by what timepiece did the whistleblower set his own watch? Imagine the hopeless contradiction if the man who determines when to blow the whistle sets his own watch by the time when the whistle is blown! Without an objective standard to judge by, no one can tell the correct time—and without an objective standard for true worth, no one can determine true value.

On what, then, should we spend life's precious ounces of energy? The common, subjective value system of our society has all the price tags reversed and is destroying our society, our children, our churches, even our faith. Before it is too late, we must untangle these mixed-up price tags and reassign them according to God's standard in His Word.

When we examine Christ's teachings, we see how far off base we are from His standards and values. It becomes obvious, then, that one of the major tasks of a church's educational ministry must be the clear teaching of values based on the authority of God's Word. This book will help you accomplish this task.

Values Defined

What exactly are values? How do values and morals interact? In his book, *Rights, Wrongs, and In-Betweens*, Jim Larson defines a value as "something that has relative worth, utility, or importance; something intrinsically valuable or desirable."[4] In other words, a value is something that is very important to an individual. Larson continues,

> A moral is a principle of right or wrong, so moral development is the development of feelings and attitudes regarding what is right or wrong. And it is often our values—what we consider to be of great importance—that influence our feelings regarding rightness or wrongness for us in any situation.
>
> God has created every person to be a valuing creature. We all prefer some things in terms of usefulness or general worth over others. We can know and feel; we can also value.
>
> Values can be expressed in everything from preference in foods to tastes in music, politics, friends, careers, leisure activities, and religious beliefs.
>
> And values do not seem to be established permanently in life, never to be modified and changed. As people grow and mature, so do their values and preferences. What people value one year may or may not be exactly what is important to them the next. . . . They say you have to be dead really to be value neutral. Promoting the idea that there are no plain moral facts is really not to understand or to be able to observe the reality of life.[5]

A more technical definition of values, but one very important for us to consider, is given to us in seven stages by Raths, Harmin, and Simon in their book *Values and Teaching*.[6] These researchers do not claim a Christian worldview, yet just as a non-Christian scientist can make accurate observations about the growth of a tree, so these studies reveal helpful insights about the development of values which takes place in an orderly, God-ordained pattern in all persons.

As Christians, we can benefit from looking at this research and applying biblical principles to it. Keep in mind, as you review the stages below, that we are offering an application of these principles based upon a Christian worldview.

1. Choosing freely. "If something is in fact to guide one's life, whether or not authority is watching, it must be a result of free choice." For Christians to choose a value freely means to choose only what is in keeping with or does not violate biblical moral standards, for Christians strongly adhere to the belief that there are biblical absolutes. Such moral choices may not be easy choices, but Jesus urged people who said they wanted to follow Him to first of all "estimate the cost" (Luke 14:28). Joshua said to Israel in the Old Testament, "choose for yourselves this day whom you will serve" (Josh. 24:15)—or which values you will serve.

2. Choosing from among alternatives. "The definition of values is concerned with things that are chosen by the individual and, obviously, there can be no choice if there are no alternatives from which to choose." The authors appropriately state that a value can never genuinely be owned unless there is a valid choice to be made. Certain alternatives, while acceptable to the world, cannot be valued by the Christian because they contradict God's holy standards. The apostle Paul urged believers to "test everything. Hold on to the good" (1 Thess. 5:21).

3. Choosing after thoughtful consideration of the consequences of each alternative. "Impulse or thoughtless choices do not lead to values as we define them. For something intelligently and meaningfully to guide one's life, it must emerge from a weighing and an understanding." Of course the Bible gives us plenty of alternatives and many strong guidelines about their consequences. (In the matter of consequences, God has the advantage of being able to see the end from the beginning.) The teacher's role is a significant one at this point because we should not only define values but also lead learners to recognize and consider the consequences of making an improper choice. The book of Proverbs is replete with admonitions regarding consequences—"Make level paths for your feet and take only ways that are firm" (Prov. 4:26).

4. Prizing and cherishing. "When we value something, it has a positive tone. We prize or cherish it, esteem it, respect it, and hold it dear. We are happy with our values." Christians give testimony to the things that they cherish, but more importantly, they *live out* their values. It was said of the apostles Peter and John that even unbelievers "took note that these men had been with Jesus" (Acts 4:13).

5. Affirming. "When we have chosen something freely after consideration of the alternatives and when we are proud of our choice, glad to be associated with it, we are likely to affirm that choice when asked about it. We are willing to publicly affirm our values." Paul stated, "I am not ashamed of the gospel" (Rom. 1:16).

6. Acting upon choices. "Where we have a value, it shows up in aspects of our living. We may do some reading about things we value. We are likely to form friendships or to be in organizations in ways that nourish our values. We may spend money on a choice we value. We budget time or energy for our values." Paul emphasized the importance of acting upon what we believe when he wrote, "And whatever you do, whether in word or deed, do it all in the name of the Lord Jesus" (Col. 3:17).

7. Repeating. "Where something reaches the stage of a value, it is very likely to reappear on a number of occasions in the life of a person who holds it. . . . Values tend to have a persistency, tend to make a pattern in a life." The psalmist wrote, "Give me understanding, and I will keep your law and obey it with all my heart" (Ps. 119:34).

This brief review of the seven stages in the formation of values reveals how powerful our values become in determining our behavior. A great deal of research has been done on the correlation between what people say they believe about a certain value versus how they live out their values in day-to-day behavior. The overwhelming evidence is that people will do what they really believe, not what they have been taught to *say* they believe. This fact, that values determine behavior, is just one reason why any church that is serious about obeying Christ's commission to "make disciples . . . teaching them to *obey* everything I have commanded you" (Matt. 28:19–20, emphasis added) will want to make values education a primary thrust and emphasis in every aspect of church life.

There are more reasons, however, why every church needs to focus on teaching values. These reasons reflect the special heritage and responsibilities we have in the body of Christ.

Biblical Mandate for Values Instruction

First, there is a strong biblical mandate for values instruction. Since the beginning of the world as recorded for us in Scripture, God has told us that His children's values must agree with His values. Values have always been a focal point of the teaching of the Word of God. Statements about values are prevalent throughout the Scriptures, yet at the same time there are certain sections in the Bible that focus especially on values. The Ten Commandments, the Sermon on the Mount, the book of Proverbs, the book of James, and many other portions of Scripture give us clear guidelines for choosing and living by biblical values.

Sometimes the world's concept of biblical values seems to be that God is sitting off in heaven inventing difficult rules for people to follow so that He can watch people jump through hoops. The church needs the tools to counter this caricature with the Good News that God loves us so much that, in wisdom, He has given us values in Scripture to guide us in His perfect way and spare us much grief and pain.

The Need for a Holy Lifestyle

Second, we need to lead all believers to the place in their lives where they have a saving and intimate walk with Jesus Christ. We must help all believers possess and practice a holy lifestyle that is consistent with their faith in Jesus Christ. In Colossians 3:1 Paul was pleading with the people of Colosse to see to it ("set your hearts on") that their value system was consistent with the fact that they were in Christ. In Romans 12:2 he also urged his Christian friends to be cautious that their value systems not be conformed to the world's patterns. These admonitions and warnings, plus numerous others from Scripture, are profoundly applicable today. The church and all its educational thrust need to be diligently working toward building in the lives of its people the behavioral patterns that grow out of a biblical value system.

A strong discipling or training ministry means that we need to be concerned with what believers know, feel, and do. Believers need a solid biblical rationale that guides their behavior. Obviously, young children have not yet arrived at the point where they can give an insightful rationale for the values they own. As they grow older and develop into young adults, however, they need to build that rationale for biblical behavior into their thought processes.

Discipleship has become a popular word in the church during the last twenty years. A genuine description of discipleship in Scripture has to do with at least three general stages. First, disciples become followers of Christ as they receive Him as Savior. Second, they grow in maturity which, of course, includes joining a congregation of believers. Third, they learn to care deeply for others as they grow in their relationship with Christ. We can do a lot of good discipling in our own educational programs. Those properly discipled have their values set on biblical guidelines; thus, a good discipleship program also makes a good values-education program.

Absolute Values Increase Self-Identity

A third important reason for being concerned about an increased thrust in values education comes from the field of psychology. Educational psychologists have discovered that when students live in a values vacuum, they tend to become confused over their self-identity. In fact, even a general education tends to take on a meaningless, almost boring, atmosphere to many students when they learn in a system where there are no absolute values. After all, why bother with anything if it doesn't really matter anyway?

The community of established absolutes can be the home, the school, and the church which, working together, become that person's value-building community. How critical it is that children in their growing-up years have some insight into who they are and what really matters! If they are not part of a community with established absolutes and values lived out by its members, children most likely will be confused about who they are, why they are here on earth, and what they ought to be doing in life.

A quick look around you will readily tell the truth of this point. Our world is more confused over self-identity than ever before. So many people in our society have no moorings because they have no self-identity based on a firm community of established absolutes; we see mass confusion and carnage increasing daily in our society.

Not only does the proper values education greatly influence a person's self-confidence, but that, in turn, becomes the glue that holds a nation together. Just as an individual life without values becomes meaningless, the evidence is overwhelming that societies that loose their values fall apart.

Strong Values Build Strong Societies

Fourth, we need to be concerned with values education because it has such tremendous benefit for us as a society. As E. M. Blaiklock writes in *Christianity Today:*

> I am now going to be positive. As a historian, I assure you that Toynbee was right in this: all human cultures grow round a central core of moral ideas and ideals that command obedience, respect and general observance. There is right and there is wrong, both unquestioned. This is what is called the "ethos" of a people, of a culture.
>
> Early Rome had something called *pietas.* We have borrowed the word twice as "piety" and "pity," neither of which represent the old Roman version of virtue and main stay of society: a loyalty to family and state, a courageous sense of duty, trustiness. Try the truth of this in all societies. Some central core holds all together.
>
> Israel had its Decalogue, its Ten Commandments and all that framed and applied them. The Commandments were stern, brief and authoritative: *Thou shalt not.* Israel also envisaged a "covenant," a promise of God conditioned by man's obedience. Historian and prophet were full of the theme: hold to the covenant and a nation stands; break it and a nation dies. Hear the somber poetry of the great Isaiah from his twenty-fourth chapter:
>
> > The earth dries up and withers,
> > The whole earth withers and grows sick,
> > And the earth itself is desecrated by the feet
> >   of those who live in it,
> > Because they have broken the laws, disobeyed the statutes and
> >   violated the eternal covenant.
> > For this curse has devoured the earth
> > And its inhabitants stand aghast.
> > For this, those that inhabit the earth dwindle.[7]

In our nation the daily headlines record the consequences of a society that no longer values its own values. When we guide our students to have biblical values, we are truly making them light and salt in a topsy-turvy world. They will become the ethos that holds America together. Isn't that the true purpose for the churches? The presence of the church of Jesus Christ in every generation has been the source of stability in our society.

TV Shapes Our Values

Fifth, numerous books and articles have informed us that television is the strongest influence on our values. Television sets are in almost every living room and often in every other room as well.

One of many volumes that illustrate the powerful influence of television on our culture is Marie Winn's *The Plug-In Drug*. Winn clearly demonstrates that under the influence of TV, we are a drugged people and therefore have little control over our senses. Anyone who walks the streets of America is greatly influenced by that powerful force, whether they personally watch TV or not.[8]

The TV industry actively reinforces a heart already gone the way of evil. Whether it initiates or only propagates our nation's morals, it is something to be reckoned with and has become the dominant pacesetter of America's morals and values. American churches and Christian education programs must counteract TV's damaging influence on all of us.

The Gap Between Knowledge and Behavior

The sixth reason we need to strengthen values education has to do with a tremendous gap between biblical knowledge and contemporary lifestyle among the American church. Roy Zuck and Gene Getz in their book *Christian Youths: An In-Depth Study* show that there is basically no correlation between what is taught in the classroom and the lifestyles of Christian youth.[9] Further studies indicate that the same lack of consistency occurs among adults. Perhaps this gap is a consequence of trying to establish values by persuasive arguments, emotional pleas, rules and regulations, religious dogma, and appeals to the conscience. Amid all of these *words,* we have not taken strong steps in *guiding the behavior* of all our church people.

This gap between beliefs and behaviors comes at a dangerous time for America. Michael W. McConnell, an expert in constitutional law and religious freedom, expresses grave concern that even the court system in America is gradually taking away not the right to *have* beliefs, but the right to *act* on those beliefs.[10]

Christ taught His disciples by personally modeling the Christian lifestyle. His example demonstrates to us that Christian values are most accurately learned when, in a sense, disciples' hands are held and they are guided through appropriate learning experiences. One of the major reasons for this book is to help teachers and leaders follow the Master's discipleship model.

Changing Family Structures

The seventh and last reason we will mention for the urgent need for concentrating on values education has to do with broken and changing families.

. . . .

In the early days of America, the family was the major communicator of absolutes and ethics, but today that is no longer the case. Because so many in America have forgotten this biblical mandate, our families—the bedrock of our society—are breaking apart, and no one is teaching our children to put their trust in God.

The psalmist understood the importance of the family as communicator of values when he said,

> We will not hide them from their children;
>   we will tell the next generation
> the praiseworthy deeds of the LORD,
>   his power, and the wonders he has done.
> He decreed statues for Jacob
>   and established the law in Israel,
> which he commanded our forefathers
>   to teach their children,
> so the next generation would know them,
>   even the children yet to be born,
>   and they in turn would tell their children.
> Then they would put their trust in God
>   and would not forget his deeds
>   but would keep his commands.
> They would not be like their forefathers—
>   a stubborn and rebellious generation,
> whose hearts were not loyal to God,
>   whose spirits were not faithful to him.
>   (Psalm 78:4–8)

Notes

1. Tony Campolo, *The Success Fantasy* (Wheaton, Ill.: Victor Books, 1980, 1993).
2. Malcolm Muggeridge, "Muggeridge Won't Slow Down," *Denver Post,* 5 April 1986.
3. William Bennett, *The De-Valuing of America: The First for Our Culture and Our Children* (Colorado Springs: Focus on the Family, 1994), quoted in *Christianity Today* (13 September 1993): 31.
4. Jim Larson, *Rights, Wrongs, and In-Betweens* (Minneapolis: Augsburg Press, 1984), 13.
5. Larson, *Rights, Wrongs, and In-Betweens,* 14.
6. Louis E. Raths, Merrill Harmin, and Sidney B. Simon, *Values and Teaching* (Columbus, Ohio: Charles E. Merrill Publishing Co., 1966), 260–61.
7. E. M. Blaiklock, *Christianity Today* (7 May 1976).
8. Marie Winn, *The Plug-In Drug* (New York: Bantam Books, 1980), chap. 2.
9. Roy B. Zuck and Gene Getz, *Christian Youth: An In-Depth Study* (Chicago: Moody Press, 1968), chap. 12.
10. Michael W. McConnell, interviewed in *The Rocky Mountain News,* 31 July 1994.

Chapter Two

. . . .

Helping People to Be Intentional About Their Values

When we speak of helping people to be intentional about their values, what do we really mean? The thesaurus yields the following synonyms for *intentional:* "premeditated," "deliberate," "contemplated," "studied," "willful," and "voluntary." Being intentional about our values refers to the aspect of choice, or free will, covered in the seven components of the definition of values in chapter 1. It is the intent of this book to help develop the early stages of values in children and then to help adults become intentional about their values.

Christians are admonished, "set your minds on things above, not on earthly things" (Col. 3:2). Moral behavior is an essential ingredient in the Christian life, even though American morality continues to decline. A number of creative educational psychologists are helping us understand better how to teach values to both children and adults. By knowing techniques and applying them appropriately as the occasion demands, we can be co-laborers with God in the lives of those entrusted to our care.

In her book *Teaching for Moral Growth,* Bonnidell Clouse reviews the work of Piaget, who closely observed children and described stages of growth children go through.

> Piaget saw moral development as proceeding from *heteronomy*, or the constraint of an external authority, to *autonomy*, or self-rule. . . . If spiritual growth is to take place, Christians must study God's word for themselves and decide which doctrinal beliefs to keep and which ones to reject. Even as children who proceed from heteronomy to autonomy, they must come to their own conclusion as to what is right and what is wrong. The process of heteronomy and autonomy might mingle and overlap, more or less, as believers accept some external constraints while internal controls are developing.[1]

. . . .

As we preach and teach the Word of God, Paul admonishes us to work together with the Holy Spirit. He states in Colossians 1:29 that we can "strive together with the working of the Spirit." If we understand how the Spirit works in people's minds, then we can certainly aid the Spirit in helping people to internalize and be intentional about their values.

Bonnidell Clouse outlines beautifully for us what our objectives will be in the learning activities.

> We will teach that victory over conflict is possible, that the behaviors we engage in are to be acceptable in the sight of God, that our thoughts, and words that express those thoughts, are known by our Creator and that the potential we have by virtue of being human comes from our redeemer rather than from ourselves. In Christ is the ultimate and complete expression of what it means to be moral. He is our model. He is our teacher.[2]

Outline for Success

The following suggestions provide some secrets to success for those who want to be strong facilitators in the valuing process.

1. Values must be modeled. The wisdom of the ages tells us that children as well as adults are influenced in what they tend to do by observing what those around them do, especially those for whom they feel admiration and affection. Nicholas Wolterstorff in his book *Educating for Responsible Action* reviews extensive research into the importance of modeling.

> It is clear from this study and a number of others like it that an adult model's standards and patterns of self reward significantly influence those of a child. The evidence seems to be that not only do the model's low standards influence the student to lower the standards which otherwise he or she would adopt, but also a model's *high* standards influence the child to *raise* his or hers. However, the self-denial induced by a stringent model gives way rather readily when the subject is confronted by another model with lower standards. . . .
>
> The decisive determinant of how the children would act was always the *action* of the model. The children tended to practice as a model practiced and *preach as the model preached!* . . . Preaching induced *preaching* rather than practice.[3]

We believe Paul was saying and demonstrating it more simply when he talked to the church in 1 Thessalonians 2:8–9.

> We loved you so much that we were delighted to share with you not only the gospel of God but our lives as well, because you had become so dear to us. Surely you remember, brothers, our toil and hardship; we worked night and day in order not to be a burden to anyone while we preached the gospel of God to you.

No wonder the church at Thessalonica had such marvelous values that they tended to turn their world upside down for Christ. Paul's life demonstrated what he was teaching.

All the research shows that the parents and significant role models in each person's life are the ones who most influence the development of that person's value system.

2. Storytelling influences values. Research on valuing suggests that storytelling has been the most effective way known of getting across a moral lesson. Jesus certainly illustrated this truth.

Storytelling is so effective in teaching lessons because stories catch our attention, entertain while they instruct, and continue to catch the imagination of the people hearing the story as the plot unfolds. It really doesn't seem to make any difference if the story is fact, fiction, religious or secular, short or long, written or oral. What matters most is that the narrative mode of the tale is able to communicate a moral lesson that remains in the listener's heart and memory. Using Scripture and teaching morality in the context of a story intensifies the values that are being taught.

Those who have studied communication throughout the centuries have found that storytelling plays a major role in communicating the values of all societies. It is interesting to note that narrative preaching is once again becoming popular. Storytelling from the pulpit powerfully conveys both biblical truths and biblical lifestyles.

3. Participation by the learner plays a key role in values internalization. It is important that a teacher-facilitator devises ways for learners to take strong, active roles in the learning process. This activity, of course, can come in many different forms. Here is a list of some of the more important ones.

a. Dilemmas, tensions, and disequilibrium. One of the major differences between an adult's mind and a child's mind is that a child can simultaneously own two different opinions without any conflict. Once a person goes through puberty, however, that ability changes. An adult cannot agree with two things that contradict each other and believe that both are true. In other words, adults cannot believe stealing and cheating are wrong and at the same time freely, without any guilt, do it. Adults will rationalize one opinion away so that their minds won't be in disequilibrium.

Before the Spirit comes into a life, a person holds only the world's view of life; it is easy to believe the world's way because there is no conflicting view in the mind. When the Spirit of God comes into a life, however, He creates a tension. John 16:8 states that "when he comes, he will convict the world of guilt in regard to sin and righteousness and judgment." If we, as facilitators, are to work in cooperation with the Spirit, we will be aware of that tension in our learners' minds. We will even try to create tension in their minds so that they will choose the values that are consistent with Scripture. We need to help them see that their views might be different from Scripture and that wrong choices will have serious consequences. When they come to that conclusion themselves, they are more apt to deal with that conflict. In *Moral Development*, Ronald Duska and Mariellen Whelan tell a story to help us in understanding the process:

> An analogy might help to understand how one reaches this "outside society perspective," this standpoint of some natural self. Imagine that there is a primitive society without contact with the outside world, since the group is completely surrounded by mountains and other societies are inaccessible for all practical purposes. We need very little anthropological knowledge to realize that this group will be highly organized according to a system of rules and taboos. These rules will be enforced with sanctions, either natural or conventional. Suppose also that the tribe believes (with no basis in fact) that not attending the ritual makes a member infectious to the other members, and thus they ostracize such an offender from the group for a period of a month, thereby never verifying the existence of the mysterious infectious powers. Now, suppose one of the members of the tribe, having violated the taboo, is ostracized. While being ostracized, he climbs up the mountain and discovers a path to another valley. Going down he encounters a new tribe with practices he has never seen before. They require no mandatory attendance at rituals and do not end up being infected by him. They perform practices which are forbidden in his tribe while outlawing practices which are perfectly normal for his tribe. Now, if he left his own valley absolutely convinced that the rules of his tribe were universal, that is, were the best rules for the society (and why should he not assume that, since he had encountered no other sets of rules?), what would this experience do to him? It would make him aware of the fact that not everything he thought to be the law was necessarily the law. He would be exposed to other ways of doing things. These other ways did not lead to chaos. Would he not then become skeptical of the correctness of his own tribe's rules? Would he not also become skeptical of the correctness of the foreign tribe's rules? Would he not begin to wonder about the best or ideal ways of behaving? The magical hold that his picture of the proper order of things had over him would be broken, unless, of course, he viewed these strange people as monsters.
>
> Let us suppose, further, that he left that valley to return home to enlighten his people as to their stupidity in some matters, but took a different passage and encountered yet another tribe with other practices, would he not begin to view the rules of each society as relative to the beliefs and needs of that society? Would not a relativism begin to develop?[4]

The role of questioning in this kind of scenario is extremely important to get people to think through the fact that they may believe a value that contradicts itself or contradicts Scripture and/or contradicts their behavior.

Dilemmas, tensions, and disequilibrium are most helpful as learning devices when learners themselves come to the conclusion that their behavior contradicts

Scripture (or even their own consciences). Rather than assuming the commanding, corrective role, the teacher-facilitator learns to ask questions that cause learners to recognize the tensions themselves.

b. Questions. As you browse through the catalog of learning activities, you will notice many of them are geared toward asking questions of the participants. A values-oriented leader will work diligently to make certain that the participants' rational processes are stimulated. The leader will stimulate their minds in such a fashion that cognitive disequilibrium will cause them to think more diligently through the issues at hand. For this reason, questions that relate to "why" issues need to be prominent in all the values exercises.

Look at the list of questions in Appendix 5, "Clarifying Responses Suggested by the Seven Valuing Processes." Try pinning this list on the refrigerator door and using it as a guideline in dialogue with your family. This type of questioning will help you and your family as you learn the reasons behind your values.

Appendix 3 is entitled "Thirty Clarifying Responses." These questions stimulate reason and thought in such a way as to alter a person's behavioral pattern. Learning to actively use these questions is essential to modifying behavior patterns.

Clouse gives us a strong example of the significance of this process.

> Asking the child questions such as "How would you feel if everyone in the family yelled shut up at you like you just did to your brother?" or "Did everyone have a good time at the party?"
>
> If a student steals, you ask him a question like "How has this practice already affected your life?" or "Are you saying that you believe that to take things that aren't really yours is an acceptable practice?" You might even ask the question, "What would be the affect in a community which is filled with people who take anything which they choose?" It is so important to look through the Gospels at the type of questions Jesus used in His dialogues with the numerous people He encountered in His pilgrimage.[5]

When using these sorts of questions, it is important to maintain an attitude of free inquiry toward the child rather than a tone of blame or accusation. Otherwise, the child will become defensive, and the elements of thoughtfully considering and freely choosing will be lost. Jesus' friendly, inquiring dialogue with the woman at the well in John 4 is a classic example of how to stimulate thought in a manner that penetrates without threatening or intimidating.

c. Making decisions. The definition of a value from chapter 1 helps us understand that people need to make their own decisions before the value really becomes their own. It is not bad for very young children to make a decision based more on coercion (for example, using decent table manners), but later that decision must become their own. Adults who want to be accepted in polite society continue to use good table manners that their parents formerly coerced, and they might even be grateful for the habit training they received when young. In the same fashion, children who become Christians in the early years of life must eventually come to the place of making that decision to follow Christ of their own volition. If they don't, their Christian lives will be very weak, because they will be unable to make appropriate choices in different, grown-up situations. Ideally, at each new stage of development, the maturing child renews the choice to follow Christ.

One of the best ways to facilitate this decision-making process is the type of exercise called a "values auction." You will find examples of these exercises listed in the catalog of activities that follows.

The secret to making a good decision is making a decision based on sound, theological, biblical reasoning. The great tendency, of course, is to tell people what decision they ought to make (and why!), rather than letting them think through their own reasoning. As the research demonstrates, this is a common, but fatal, error.

To be a creative activity designer, you will want to incorporate into the learning design some component that will force your participants not only to make sound decisions but also to articulate the reasons behind those decisions.

d. Learning by playing. Well, everyone ought to really enjoy this one! This is the one that sounds like the most fun. Let's learn a little bit about play from an article in the resource sheet called *UpDate,* published by the Christian Education department of the national office of the Covenant Church.

> "[T]he deepest realization of man's humanity occurs in power-free, sincerely creative play." The ability to play, especially as an adult, requires a great amount of freedom and maturity. That person who can play can also cope with life positively. He has developed the skills to handle the surprising and the mundane creatively and through it all is convinced that life is worth celebrating. . . .
>
> Play is a positive response to life. It is chosen freely and involves risk and achievement. The player must be motivated by desire to experience and enjoy life. Play challenges one to make choices, exercising the power of decision. Above all, play is fun! It isn't a shallow response to life. It is a freedom to respond fully.
>
> Because play involves freedom, a liberated state of mind must be realized before creative play can take place. This is one reason play is easily associated with children and so difficult to achieve as adults.[6]

If you are going to have your participants engage in play, you will want to make certain that they can experiment with a certain amount of freedom so that they will try new ideas. The scholars say that children learn more when they are free in having fun, but, actually, adults do the same. The problem for adults is that many of them have not played as adults and may find it difficult. You will find numerous activities in the catalog leaning towards fun and play, but you will notice that there is always an element of decision making and trust building included in each game.

· ·

Helping People to Be Intentional About Their Values

4. Social interaction needs to occur in a just, moral community. Bonnidell Clouse reminds us tersely, "If we grow up in a good environment, we learn to be good. If we grow up in a bad environment, we learn to be bad. In other words, we learn to be what we are made to be by the environmental conditions in which we find ourselves."[7]

Both the Old and the New Testaments generally reinforce this concept, although God can work in a person's life regardless of the environment. A just moral community greatly facilitates the learning process. The following study illuminates the role of the community in facilitating the development of a value tendency.

1.	Mutual respect	1 Thessalonians 4:9–10, Ephesians 2:14, James 2:1–3
2.	A sense of belonging	Ephesians 1:4–5
3.	Experiences of justice	Colossians 3:12, Matthew 18:15–17, Philippians 2:14–15
4.	Openness about moral concerns (discussions)	Hebrews 10:24, 1 Thessalonians 4:1–2, Acts 10
5.	Experiences of social integration	Ephesians 4:15–16, Acts 2:46

Our congregation went through a very traumatic experience recently when we had to exercise church discipline. Every child and adult who observed and interacted in that process learned the importance of corporate discipline. Every congregation that is serious about being a New Testament church will not only teach the need for discipline, but will also practice it. It is not only what a community or group does that is proper, but also what it does improperly that teaches either good or evil. Some of the greatest lessons we learn as believers are from the ways congregations both model and deal with sin and righteousness. Growing Christians need to see how we deal with our people and the norms and procedures we demonstrate in the everyday practice of living out the life of the church of Jesus Christ.

5. Encouragement reinforces a value. In the book of Acts, Barnabas was given the nickname son of *paraklēsis,* that is, "son of encouragement," because he was always building up other people. You remember that the Holy Spirit is called a *paraclete* meaning "one who comes alongside to encourage." The word is translated many ways in the New Testament but generally means to encourage. Encouragement is a key element in the discipling process.

Watch a father helping his young daughter learn to ride her two-wheeled bike. He tells her how, puts her on the bike, and runs alongside while she tries to pedal and steer. He keeps uttering words of encouragement, "You are doing great! Keep it up!" Finally, she learns to ride on her own and feels joy and satisfaction in her accomplishment.

A discipling teacher identifies with that father by telling students or participants how to live a godly life and then running alongside them, as Barnabas did with Paul, all the time giving them encouragement—"You can make it! Why not go back and try it again!" In order to "paraclete" people, you need to get involved in their lives and urge them along the way in their spiritual development. This encouragement is vital for the learner's self-esteem. Once the daughter learns to ride the bike, she feels very good about herself. The father will hear about it for many days and in many different ways.

Once adults learn new values and are encouraged in the process by a support group, they tend to feel better about themselves. We have had the joy of playing a major role as facilitators in that value-learning process. As you study the various activities in the catalog, notice how many of them call for the role of the "paraclete," or the encourager.

As you continue to use the values exercises in this book—and create additional ones—keep in mind the guidelines listed in this chapter. You will become an excellent facilitator, causing others to learn and internalize the values of Christ's disciples.

Notes

1. Bonnidell Clouse, *Teaching for Moral Growth* (Wheaton, Ill.: Victor Books, 1993), 224.
2. Clouse, *Teaching*.
3. Nicholas Wolterstorff, *Educating for Responsible Action* (Grand Rapids: Eerdmans, 1980), 55–57.
4. Ronald Duska and Mariellen Whelan, *Moral Development* (New York: Paulist Press, 1975), 70.
5. Clouse, *Teaching*.
6. *UpDate*, published by the Christian Education Department of the National Office of the Covenant Church, 1 April 1975.
7. Clouse, *Teaching*.

Chapter Three

. . . .

Guides for Using Valuing Activities

When a value is internalized, it becomes part of the very fiber of the person's soul. It is such a strong force that it guides all of the major decisions in the person's life. If you are genuinely concerned about discipling others, you will be extremely interested in helping them internalize a biblical set of values. Good disciplers will be very dependent on the Holy Spirit's guidance to help them be creative as they disciple others.

This book's extensive inventory of value-building exercises will help you become an effective, value-building discipler. You will want to be very creative in the use of these exercises. Each group of people will be different, so we hope that you will choose those exercises which best suit your particular group's needs and modify them for your group as necessary.

What are some possible uses for these exercises? They can be used for Sunday school sessions, leadership training times, home schooling, adult retreats, Vacation Bible School, women's fellowship groups, camps, and Christian day schools. Some will aid you in building a meaningful and growing experience in your discipleship or covenant groups. Whatever your group is called or whatever the size, there will be an aid here to help you make disciples of Jesus Christ. We pray that as you use them, you will better understand the structure of a good valuing activity so that in time you will be able to develop many yourself.

This selection of activities is composed of exercises from both of the authors' covenant group experiences and from the exercises created by many Denver Seminary students for a course on values education. Still others are selections from various magazines and books.

In order to get the most benefit out of these value exercises, here are some important facts and principles to keep in mind.

. . . .

Make it clear that the exercise is worth their effort

You need to answer the unspoken question in every student's mind, "Why should I bother with this at all?" Participants must come to see the tremendous value of each exercise in order to give themselves sufficiently to integrate that value into their lives. Students will give themselves to the task in proportion to their ability to see its worth. When using a valuing exercise with a group to teach a Bible lesson, for example, you'll find that people will give themselves in proportion to what Larry Richards calls being "hooked."

For instance, if you are going to teach a young child the importance of sharing what he has with friends, you will need to start out by helping him see the extreme importance of having friends. Preschool children might be motivated to learn this value because they see the great benefit of having a host of friends. In contrast, toddlers, who are not yet developmentally mature enough to enjoy cooperative play with other toddlers, are notoriously resistant to learning to share! In the end, developmental growth causes the once-selfish, now "mature" four-year-old to want to share with playmates because he has learned to see the worth of friends.

Be specific

When you define the exact purpose for the exercise, make sure that it is a narrowly focused purpose. If it is too broad, it really won't take because people generally are not able to apply the broader principles to the specific objective. For instance, if you try to teach the value of respect for others, it may be too broad. It is better to start with learning to respect members of one's family. A key principle to remember here is: People are more apt to go from the specific to the general rather than from the general to the specific.

Know your learners' abilities

As you introduce the valuing exercise to others, make sure that the people you are targeting are able to comprehend the truth. If you want an effective value-teaching ministry to children, it is imperative to educate yourself about the normal milestones of their intellectual growth, so that you know what is reasonable to expect of a given age group. You must make sure your audience has matured intellectually and rationally enough to practice and to understand the reasoning behind the value. If you want learners to own (internalize) the value, then it is very important that they have the developmental capacity to understand the value.

Toddlers, for example again, have not yet matured into the developmental phase where their young minds can comprehend time. For them, everything is "now." They cannot make a decision about the future since they cannot perceive what future commitment is all about. Their world is too small. Even if you could get a toddler to comprehend today that it's unkind to pull the dog's tail, it is impossible to get a moral commitment out of a toddler not to pull the dog's tail tomorrow.

We can draw another example from junior high students. At this age, children are starting to move from concrete to more abstract thought. Most stories using literary devices such as metaphors to symbolize meanings will get a literal interpretation from a roomful of ten-year-olds, while a class of sixteen-year-olds will be much more likely to catch the deep inner meaning. Since girls mature more rapidly than boys during junior high, you may find all the girls catching on to the abstract concepts while the boys are secretly wondering what it is all about. Naturally, they will not admit that something is passing them by! Their preferred response may be to keep the class more interesting on their own level by distracting with humor or misbehavior.

Aim for increased knowledge and changed behavior

As you think about the objective for the valuing activity, ask yourself the key question: Is this valuing exercise intended to build a tendency in one's life or is it basically a means of helping one gather data or information? Does it cause a development of a tendency toward a new, godly behavior, or are you expecting them to just have some new knowledge at the completion of the exercise? Psalm 119:66 says, "Teach me knowledge and good judgment, for I believe in your commands." The psalmist says we do need to have a knowledge base, but that knowledge base must lead to good judgment. That is how a value is internalized. Eventually, a good knowledge base leads to good judgment, which expresses itself in improved behavior.

A leader's goal must be to facilitate learning

Hebrews 10:24 tells us to stir up one another to love and good works. It is not just the leader's task to give out information. As leaders, our task is to change lives and change behaviors. To aid in that process the leader must play the role of a facilitator. Yes, the discipler-leader must give out information when and where needed and provide the necessary guidance into the experience which will cause change.

How do we play the facilitator role? When we provide direction and engage in dialogue, we stir up cognitive (and emotional) disequilibrium. This disequilibrium, or tension, stimulates the ones being discipled to seriously think through their behavior and its accompanying rationale. The facilitator encourages the participants to look at their normal behavior and logic and then decide for themselves how they are going to live their lives, whether or not they will choose any changes in how they live.

A facilitator's role primarily is to cause another person to choose—make a decision. The facilitator does not necessarily respond to everything that is said but makes sure that as a whole the group is engaged in a process that ultimately will accomplish the internalization of a particular value. A facilitator is one who asks questions, challenges responses, and gets the group members to interact.

Good facilitators are very cautious and do not threaten people or answer their own questions. The task is to put folks at ease, not to force them to answer questions with preconceived responses.

Participants must make the decision to change for themselves; facilitators continually need to encourage honesty and insight on the part of the participants and make sure that participants understand all possible alternatives.

Flexibility and creativity

It is important to keep in mind that the value responses are not mechanical things that follow a formula. You will be a great facilitator if you strengthen the group's creative muscles and help members gain insight into themselves and their values. Don't encourage them always to color within the lines. Sometimes, greater creativity comes when they learn to draw their own lines and color in a creative way outside those lines. In the same way, you don't always have to stay within prescribed instructions given for a particular exercise. You may find a more creative and individualized way to accomplish the given task.

You, like the people who designed the activities in this workbook, will learn to create new and special learning exercises by blending the parts and putting the pieces together in ways that are custom-tailored to your needs.

When you think of creativity, you think of fun and adventure. Take your participants where they have never been before. Make them think through things they have never thought before, and cause them to interact with others as they have never done before. Creativity brings zest to learning!

Participants must understand the process

In working with groups, one finds that participants quickly forget verbal instructions or inappropriately apply them. It is so important, as the group goes to start the activity, that they have something in hand (or on a board or chart) that exactly describes what questions they are to answer and what processes they are to follow. It is amazing how people quickly forget instructions! The clearer the instructions, the more certain that the objective will be accomplished.

Use visuals to enrich the activity

The white board, chalk board, charts, transparencies, handouts, toys, and other objects richly enhance learning experiences. Often you will note that speakers who have an object in hand as they teach find the audience interacting with them more readily. Research shows that an audience often remembers the lesson's objective longer when they associate that objective with something visual. That is certainly true of values education. Our minds do tend to associate meaning with objects. It's worth your time and effort to dig out some props and dream up ways to use these objects.

Be patient with timing

As you start the activity, make sure to plan for adequate time for the exercise to take place. Values activities are significantly different from lectures. Lectures are word intensive and value activities are participant intensive. You give the lecture and hope and pray that people interact mentally with the things you said. Likewise, it takes time for a valuing exercise to leave an impression on the learners' minds—and even longer to become part of their lives.

It is of primary importance that each group member goes through the rationale-developing process that internalizes the value. Some will go through this process more quickly than others; you must allow time for people to interact with the experience within their own time frames. Each mind must be challenged. If you want to either change their value structure (reasoning) or intensify their convictions on a certain value, then you must develop in them a tendency toward behaving in the new way. In order to develop these new behaviors, you might encourage disagreement or cause the group to carefully evaluate their statements. On other occasions you might challenge them so that they will ultimately either come to agree with you or come to thoroughly understand why they do not.

It is very helpful, after teaching a value, to review what has been learned. This review tends to reinforce the value, building it more firmly into the behavior patterns.

Include social interaction

It is helpful to hear where others are in their thinking. If they are going to disagree with the norm established by the group, then they need to think through why they are disagreeing and whether or not that is an appropriate or worthwhile position to hold.

Because peers are so important in the learning process, mutual respect, a sense of belonging, and an atmosphere of justice must be established by the leader each time you use a values exercise. Reflect a moment and you will see how, for new believers, wholesome experiences within the church can be a vital support in the development of a new value. Then when you see a person living out a value in society, you know it has been internalized.

Summarize to make it last

As active, creative, and even fun as the valuing exercise may be, it is not complete unless participants experience a moment of reflection. In order for students to consolidate and take home the benefits of the exercise, time to summarize is essential. Learners need to verbalize for themselves and to each other what they learned through the process. You need to put in writing the conclusions, the reactions, and the observations of the group. The more people you can get to participate in the summarization process, the better it will be. Use "couple buzzers" or small groups. Talk with them about the structure of a value and the reasoning behind it. Write the answers on a white board or chalk board or have each person write down his or her own conclusions on a piece of paper. The value at hand is more apt to become a genuine part of the daily experiences when it is summarized.

Exercises for Youth
. . . .

Exercise One

. . . .

Healthy Hearing

by Mark Rich

Age: High School

Setting: An informal group in an area where noise is not a problem

Time: 45 minutes

Goal: To give students an opportunity to become more aware of the content of the music they listen to and to value what goes into their ears (This moves them into the stage of choosing thoughtfully and reflectively, see pp. 8–9)

Leader Preparation: Announce well in advance that students can bring some of their favorite music to class; a variety of tapes and CDs of your own, including: classical, country, soft pop, rock and roll, heavy metal, etc.; a tape/CD player; pencils and writing pads for all students and a Bible and concordance.

Scripture: Romans 8:5–6; 2 Corinthians 6:14–18; Galatians 6:7–8

The Exercise:
1. Gather the group around the tape player, with writing pads in hand.
2. Play a variety of styles of music and have participants write down their choices (best and worst) and the reasons for their choices.
3. Next, play some of the most popular songs of the day. Pause occasionally, if necessary, to catch the words. Have the students write down the core message in each song you play.

Summary and Conclusion:
Summarize with a discussion using these questions:
1. What values did we hear in _____ (a specific piece)?
2. On the board, list the songs you heard and try to summarize with a word or phrase the values each presents.
3. Do any patterns emerge? (For example, are all country songs about

. . . .

alcohol and lost love? Are all heavy metal songs about instant gratification?)

4. Ask the group: Is it possible to hear music on a continuous basis without picking up the message—even if the words *are* hard to hear?
5. Is the message in any of the music consistent with biblical values? If so, which music and which values?
6. Is there any way to enjoy a certain type of music and get a good message at the same time?
7. What are some alternatives available that offer good quality music and a message that does not run counter to biblical values?
8. How will what music you listen to this week be different as a result of this study?

Conclude with reading Romans 8:5–9; 2 Corinthians 5:14–18; Galatians 6:7–8, and prayer.

Exercise Two

Traits I Value

by Susie Hayes

Age: Junior High or High School

Setting: Individual or group

Time: 20–30 minutes

Goal: Using a self-evaluation tool, allow students to explore how they measure themselves on specific character traits

Leader Preparation: Focusing on You survey (p. 31) and pencil for each participant

Scripture: Psalm 139:1–6, 23–24

The Exercise:
A. Introduce the Focusing on You survey by asking: Do you really know yourself? What makes you special and unique? What are your strong and weak areas? How do you see yourself?
B. Hand out the surveys and allow a few minutes for students to complete them.
C. Lead a discussion, using some of the following questions:
   1. How did it feel to use this survey? Did you feel awkward about having to judge yourself? Perhaps some of you felt like failures because you had to acknowledge you aren't "Really Terrific" on every item all the time. Perhaps others of you felt like boasters if you gave yourself a high rating in a specific area—even if you feel it's the truth.
   2. By looking at your response checks, do you feel you see yourself as you really are? Why?
   3. Do you think your best friend would score you the same way that you have scored yourself? How about your mom or dad? How about God?
   4. What characteristics do you feel are not important?
   5. What traits are very important?
   6. Which characteristics does God value?
   7. Select a characteristic you can work to improve or develop this week.

Summary and Conclusion:
Using 1 Corinthians 4:1–5, point out how hard it is for us humans to evaluate ourselves accurately. Conclude with Psalm 139:1–6, 23–24 and a prayer that God would search us and know us.

Focusing on You Survey

Characteristic	My Response			
	Really Terrific!	OK most of the time	Not one of my finer qualities	You've got to be kidding!
Compassionate	☐	☐	☐	☐
Generous	☐	☐	☐	☐
Responsible	☐	☐	☐	☐
Hardworking	☐	☐	☐	☐
Decisive	☐	☐	☐	☐
Authentic (real)	☐	☐	☐	☐
Caring about social issues	☐	☐	☐	☐
Interested in others	☐	☐	☐	☐
Loyal	☐	☐	☐	☐
Gifted	☐	☐	☐	☐
Superior to most others	☐	☐	☐	☐
Courageous	☐	☐	☐	☐
Intelligent	☐	☐	☐	☐
Lovable	☐	☐	☐	☐
Many pleasing mannerisms	☐	☐	☐	☐
Sense of humor	☐	☐	☐	☐
Grateful	☐	☐	☐	☐
Emotionally warm	☐	☐	☐	☐
Interesting	☐	☐	☐	☐
Active	☐	☐	☐	☐
Consistent	☐	☐	☐	☐
Independent	☐	☐	☐	☐
Important to others	☐	☐	☐	☐
In control of my life	☐	☐	☐	☐
Good-looking	☐	☐	☐	☐
Able to stand alone for my beliefs	☐	☐	☐	☐
Great potential	☐	☐	☐	☐

Pulling Strings

by Jeanne Williams

Age: Junior High through College

Setting: Group of 10–15

Time: About 45 minutes

Goal: To allow participants to experience the dynamics and pressures typical of parents and grandparents and to develop empathy for their feelings (Youth will be engaged in step 3 of Raths, Harmon, and Simon's steps of internalizing a value)

Leader Preparation: About 7 yards of strong string and a pair of scissors

Scripture: Malachi 4:6; 1 Peter 3:8; Matthew 18:33; Hebrews 5:2; 10:34

The Exercise:

1. Prepare the group to role-play. You are the director. Choose two persons to play a mother and a father. Set them in chairs facing each other. Tie a string from the mother's right wrist to the father's left wrist and from the father's right wrist to the mother's left wrist. Choose young people who will really get into their roles and tell them to become as emotionally involved in their roles as they can. The only rule is that whenever one wants to say something to the other, each must pull on his or her string first. Let them hear the scenario and talk through their roles before you proceed.

   Dad: Dad is a successful businessman and also very involved in the church. He wants to spend more time with his family, but whenever the pastor asks him to do something that he can do well, he feels guilty about saying no. Dad also spends a lot of time at work in order to provide for the family—if he didn't they might not have some of the nice things that they really like.

Mom: Mom wishes he would spend more time with her and the kids. During the last two weeks, he has only been home for dinner once. As we join them, Dad has just returned from work—late—and everyone is hungry and eager to eat. They have just sat down to their meal.

2. Now, select two more youngsters to play the son and the daughter. Have them sit in chairs on either side of Mom and Dad. Tie one string from each child to each parent (see diagram). Their role is to enter into the discussion as the family eats one of those rare meals together, either talking about the same thing Mom and Dad are discussing or bringing up their own things (the cute girl he just met at school, or can she go to Suzy's house for a slumber party, or whatever). They must pull the string that leads to whomever they want to talk to before they talk.

3. Allow the family to talk for several minutes while other group members observe (They can be guardian angels who are silent and invisible but interested in and caring for the family). During each stage, let the family talk until you can see some tension developing. For some role-players this may take longer than others. As the director, be ready to prompt the players with items to talk about if they are slow starters. Eventually, they should be able to role-play some spontaneous dialogue.

4. Finally, add one more person to play the mother's mother. Her string will only be tied to her daughter (the family mom), and when she wants to say something to anyone else in the family, she must relay a message to them through her daughter. The family must also go through Mom to speak to Grandma.

5. Allow the whole family to continue talking for about five more minutes, then cut all the strings loose and have the entire group sit in a circle for discussion time.

Variation: If you have only 7 or 8 participants, you could add more strings to Dad or Mom such as a Boss or Pastor phoning in the middle of the meal with requests or demands. Then each person would have a speaking role, and there would be no guardian angels.

Summary and Conclusion:
1. Encourage both the role-players and the onlooking angels to discuss their observations of the preceding play.
2. Go around the group and ask each person, "How did you feel?"
3. Also, "How do you think so-and-so felt?" or, "How would you feel in that situation? Does this remind you of anything you've experienced or observed in real life?"

4. At some point the discussion should get around to how pressured the parents felt with all the tugging that was being done and perhaps that the children felt ignored or left out. Have the "children" and the "parents" defend or explain their actions to each other.
5. Ask everyone in the group, "Did you learn anything that you did not realize about parents? about grandparents? about children? (Here you are encouraging them to express empathy for those in different roles.)
6. Encourage the group to suggest some ideas about how they could treat their family members differently in light of what they have learned about how it feels to be on the other side of the string.
7. Finally, ask each group member to think of a specific thing they might do differently today because of what they have learned.

Read Malachi 4:6.

Diagram for "Pulling Strings"

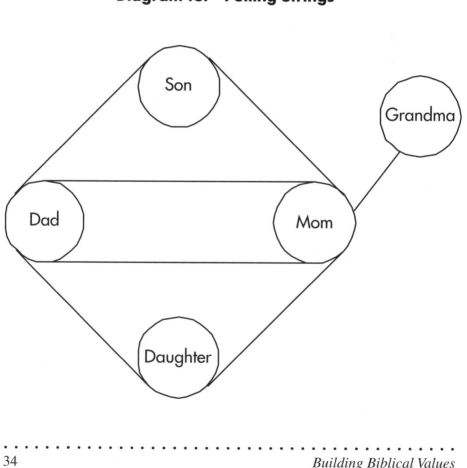

Godly Self-Esteem

by D. Yngsdal

Age: Junior High through College (but don't include that broad an age spread in the same group)

Setting: Group

Time: 30 minutes

Goal: To provide a setting in which youth can learn that it is God's will for them to value themselves as part of God's beloved creation

Leader Preparation: Bibles, pencils, and 3 x 5 cards for all students; specific Scriptures prepared for study; concordance and a black board also helpful

Scripture: Numbers 13:25–33; Proverbs 30:21–23; Romans 12:3; 1 Corinthians 3:10; 15:9–10; Philippians 1:1–26

The Exercise:

Make sure each person has a Bible, a pencil, and a 3 x 5 card. Announce you are going to take a "private survey." Have students list the following 3 statements on their cards and then mark a "+" or a "–" by each statement, depending on their answer.

1. I'm not perfect, but I generally like myself.
2. I feel that others usually value and appreciate me.
3. I consistently feel that other people like to be near me.

Two or more answers having a plus indicates that a person has a positive self-image.

Now, have the group answer the following questions, using the Scripture references available (If your group is larger than 10 people, have them break up into groups of 4 or 5).

1. Is it proper for a Christian to have a positive self-image? Read 1 Corinthians 3:10 and Philippians 1:1–26.
2. Define a proper self-image. Read Romans 12:3, 1 Corinthians 15:9–10, and Philippians 3:4–9.
3. What results come from a positive self-image? What results come from a negative self-image? Read Numbers 13:25–33 where those who saw themselves as mere "grasshoppers" lacked the courage to obey God, Proverbs 30:21–23, and Philippians 1:12–26.

Summary and Conclusion:

Ask each member of the group to decide what mental changes he or she needs to make about self-image. Have each record these changes on the reverse side of the 3 x 5 card.

Exercise Five

Create an Ending

by Richard Siemens

Age: Junior High through College

Setting: Group

Time: 20–30 minutes

Goal: To give students the opportunity to create several alternative responses to a moral dilemma about tension between respect for and justified anger toward an adult

Leader Preparation: The story ready to tell; paper, pencil, and a Bible for each group

Scripture: Matthew 18:15–17; Romans 12:16–18; Ephesians 4:2–3; 2 Timothy 2:23–25; Hebrews 10:24, or other Scriptures students can recall. A concordance is always helpful.

The Exercise:
1. Have students split up into small groups of three or four and give each group a sheet of paper. Have each group choose a "scribe" to write down ideas. This can either be a volunteer or "the one whose birthday is closest to July 4," etc.
2. Explain that you are going to tell them a story, but it will be each group's job to finish the story. They should come up with several interesting and exciting endings.
3. Next, they will need to (a) consider the consequences of each ending they created, (b) select the most biblical alternative, and (c) be prepared to tell the rest why they selected this particular ending.
4. The story:

   A person representing a social agency (for example, the Food Bank) in your neighborhood comes and speaks at your church. His message is interesting, but you feel he unjustly criticizes the youth in your community's churches for their "lack of concern for other young people." You think he is not in touch with what the youth in the churches are attempting to do. By the time he finishes, you are furious. As you leave the church, you notice that the speaker is greeting people at the door. You will have to pass him on your way out. STOP. What could you do? What should you do?
5. While students are coming up with story endings, leader writes steps a, b, and c (from step 3) on the board for them.
6. When they have finished, ask someone from each group to report their solution and why they selected it.

Summary and Conclusion:
   To conclude, have different students read some of the Bible verses to the group, either from the list at the beginning of this lesson or ones that they look up. How well do the different endings the students created line up with these verses?

Exercise Six

· ·

The World's Squeeze Box*

Age: Junior High through College

Setting: Individual Bible study, one-to-one discipleship tool, or group

Time: 60 minutes

Goal: To challenge young people to think how seriously they are influenced by the world's monetary system

Leader Preparation: Have a copy of Romans 12:1–2 from the J. B. Phillips paraphrase; pen, Bible, and A Closer Look at Values work sheet (p. 38) available for each participant

Scripture: Romans 12:1–2; 1 John 2:15–17; Matthew 6:19–21, 24–34; 19:16–30

The Exercise: Complete the worksheet.

A Closer Look at Values Work Sheet

A. Which Mold?
1. What contrasting values are presented in Romans 12:1–2?
2. List 3 ways the "world" tries to mold people (e.g., values presented in advertising). See also 1 John 2:15–17.
3. How can a person become the kind of person who has values that are more Christlike? Romans 12:1–2 will give you some beginning ideas.

---

* For additional help on this lesson, see *How to Decide What's Really Important* by Fritz Ridenour (Ventura, Calif.: Regal Books, 1978). Used by permission.

· ·

B. What's Your Motive?
1. What contrasting values are presented in Matthew 6:19–21, 24–34?
2. What does it mean to "lay up treasures on earth"?
3. What does it mean to "lay up treasures in heaven"?
4. List the pros and cons of storing up treasures on earth. Do the same for storing up treasures in heaven.
C. Internal Conflict
1. What contrasting values are presented in Matthew 19:16–30?
2. Did Jesus say it was wrong for the man to have money? What was the man's problem?
3. For the man in Matthew 19, love of money got in his way when it came to joyfully and totally obeying Christ. What values get in the way of Christian young people today when it comes to obeying Christ totally?

Summary and Conclusion:
1. Choose one of the verses from the work sheet to memorize this week.
2. What one behavior has been brought to your mind that you could commit to prayerfully examining this week?

Exercise Seven

. . . .

To Tell the Truth

by Bill van Bark

Age: Junior High through College

Setting: 10–20 participants

Time: 30–60 minutes, depending on discussion time

. . . .

Goal: To consider the value behind the rule of "tell the truth"; to aid participants in considering all the alternatives when they make decisions, either for an organization or for their personal lives. *Note:* Leader should be able to observe contrasting developmental levels of moral reasoning, depending on the age group.

Leader Preparation: Copies of When Is It Right to Let People Be Killed? (p. 41) for each participant to read, Bibles for reference

Scripture: 1 Samuel 20:33b, 21:1–10, 22:11–23

The Exercise:
   Hand out copies of When Is It Right to Let People Be Killed? After everyone has read about this dilemma, the group discusses the following questions (These questions are related to the seven valuing processes.) Keep the discussion centered on the issue of telling the truth and on instances when doing so contradicts the welfare of the majority.
   1. Was there a choice for Churchill to make regarding telling the truth?
   2. If you had been in Churchill's place, would you have made the same decision? Why or why not?
   3. What else would you consider before you made your decision? Were all possible alternatives listed in the article?
   4. What would be the consequences for each available alternative? *(Leader:* List these on the board as they are mentioned.)
   5. Was your decision a good one?
   6. Are you willing to be counted for it? *(Leader:* You may invite people to "take a stand" in different areas of the room, depending on their choice, in order to dramatize this step.)
   7. If your family were involved, would it change your decision?
   8. How did you set priorities between the different alternatives?
   9. "It is never right to do wrong in order to do right." Is this a biblical truth or not? Show the Scriptures to back up your stand.
   10. Can you think of any times in Scripture where someone concealed the truth?
   11. What does it mean to you when people talk about "playing God"? Are there some decisions only God should be trusted with? Give examples.

Summary and Conclusion:
   Conclude by reading 1 Samuel 20:33b, 21:1–10, 22:11–23, where a lie saved the lives of some but cost the lives of others, in another situation.

When Is It Right to Let People Be Killed?*

It is war. Poland, Holland, Belgium, and France have surrendered to the Nazi war machine. England is the next target. With terrible fury the Nazi air force sends its bombers to blast England into submission. London is in flaming shambles. But England will not surrender.

On the fourteenth of November, the German High Command orders an attack on the beautiful city of Coventry, with a population of nearly a quarter of a million. Through the darkness they come. The droning of engines shatters the stillness, air-raid sirens scream out their warning—too late. The bombs explode, leaving a deathly quiet over the city. Seventy thousand homes are leveled to the ground. Thousands of men, women, and children who did not make it to the air-raid shelter lie dead. The beautiful ancient churches of Coventry are smashed and scarred. England weeps.

Prime Minister Churchill comes to inspect the damage. With a stern face, cigar clenched between his teeth, he walks among the ruins. He listens as the people of Coventry describe the horror of the night. He asks questions. But he tells no one that he knew the bombing raid was coming—that he could have evacuated the city's doomed population in time.

Why would Churchill, the leader of his nation, allow his people to die when an early warning might have saved them? Because of Project Ultra—one of the most important and closely guarded secrets of World War II. Somehow Allied leaders had gotten hold of a German code machine and had learned to decipher any message sent by the German military command. The code was extremely difficult, but they had finally cracked it. From this code Churchill received the fateful message: Coventry would be bombed.

And because of this code, because of Project Ultra, the Prime Minister faced a stark dilemma: What should he do with the information? He could order the city to be evacuated immediately, have the Royal Air Force jam the navigational aids the Germans used, and take other counter measures. But doing any of these things would tell the Germans that the Allies had advance knowledge of the attack. As a precaution, they would very likely change their code system and gone would be the one great advantage the Allies had over Germany. Again and again this access to German military orders had proved to be the only thing between the Allies and defeat. Project Ultra saved the Allied forces from total destruction before Dunkirk, and it gave the Royal Air Force time to get their planes off the ground before a German bombing raid. To give away the secret of Project Ultra by evacuating Coventry might mean losing the war.

Churchill agonized over the decision. In the end he decided to do nothing except to secretly put the firefighters, police, and ambulance drivers on the alert. Human beings who could have been saved died in that raid. But it was Churchill's carefully considered opinion that to save them would endanger countless lives later and might lead to final defeat for the Allies.

---

* Jack Roeda, *Decisions* (Grand Rapids: Board of Publications of the Christian Reformed Church, 1980), 17–18.

. . . .

Exercises for Youth

Exercise Eight

· ·

TV and Me!

by Carolyn Tunnell

Age: Youth, ages 12–16

Setting: Group of 15–18

Time: 60 minutes

Goal: To help youth critically examine their television-viewing habits

Leader Preparation: Pencils or pens and a TV and Me! survey sheet (pp. 44–45) for each participant; Bibles, a calculator, and a board or large sheet of paper will be handy

Scripture: Psalm 101:3; Romans 12:2; Ephesians 4 and 5 (selected passages), 2 Timothy 3:1–5

The Exercise:

Individually:
   A. Give the students the TV and Me! survey sheet and pencils or pens.
   B. Instruct them to choose their three favorite television programs and write them on the three television sets on the left of the sheet.
   C. Next, the participants evaluate each program by checking one or two boxes on the right side of the sheet.
   D. Finally, they should answer the questions about how much they watch TV and about commercials.

As a group:
   A. When all are ready, ask them to pick some of the shows that are the most popular. Probably some of the same programs will be picked by several group members. List them on the board.
   B. Next, have the group discuss their ratings from the right side of their survey sheets. Is there any consensus in the ratings? Does the group perceive some programs as less pleasing to God than others?

· ·

C. Does the group feel that it would be possible to make a program that would be pleasing to God? Would anyone watch it?

D. Lead the group in a discussion of the following:

   1. Discuss the moral content of several programs. Establish a baseline of biblical values about lifestyle values. Use the Bible verses to clarify godly values, and challenge the youth to scan Galatians 4–5 for relevant points. Jot key phrases on the board as they come out. Now, help the group transfer this to TV. Have they ever seen any programs that feature content and lifestyle choices contrary to Scriptures just read? Which programs? Are there even programs that present these lifestyles as acceptable and absolutely normal and healthy? Have the group give specific instances.

   2. Next discuss the issue of violence. A key to this discussion is that violence is so prevalent the group may overlook it and fail to recognize the amount of violence they actually see on TV.

   3. Now, using the calculator and the figures they shared about their television-viewing habits, quickly run some composite statistics. For example:

      a) Amount of TV viewed by one person in a year
      b) Amount of TV viewed by one person since he or she was born
      c) Amount of TV viewing that could be projected into a lifetime
      d) Amount of TV viewed by this particular group for a year

      These statistics should stimulate some discussion about how people choose to use their time. What would they like to see their lives add up to? Challenge the group to come up with alternate, more attractive ways of spending time, especially if the amount of time they spend on TV is excessive.

E. Finally, focus discussion on TV advertising. What impact does this advertising have on teen lifestyles? Encourage group members to share personal experiences—both positive and negative—they have had in this regard. Have any of their experiences increased their trust for or respect for the adult world of corporations, ad agencies, and marketing?

Summary and Conclusion:

   1. Ask two or three of the more articulate group members to summarize the group's consensus on each item and invite the rest of the group to help. Jot their conclusions on the board.

   2. Ask if any think they will change any of their viewing habits this coming week. What would they do instead of watching television?

TV and Me!

My Favorite Television Programs — Write the names of your favorite programs in the television sets and then check 1 or 2 appropriate columns for each program.	Pleases God	Expresses a good lifestyle for a believer	Is neutral	Expresses a lifestyle that a believer would not want	Displeases God

Building Biblical Values

Please answer the following questions:
1. I usually watch _____ hours of television per week.
2. List two television commercials that influenced you to buy the product they advertised.
   a) Product 1 was _____

   Did you believe what you were told in the commercial?

   _____

   Was the product as good as it was advertised to be?

   _____

   b) Product 2 was _____

   Did you believe what you were told in the commercial?

   _____

   Was the product as good as it was advertised to be?

   _____

Exercise Nine

· ·

Where Your Heart Is

by Lori Seed

Age: High School

Setting: An area large enough to accommodate several "stations" and allow movement from station to station

Time: 45 minutes

Goal: To demonstrate the value of choosing spiritual disciplines over what the world offers

Leader Preparation: Create chips and envelopes for each participant. The chips are small pieces of construction paper that bear the words: *time, popularity, ability,* or *money.* (Or, use different colors of paper to color-code your chips). Each participant will receive an envelope with ten chips of each type. Also prepare a large number of extra chips to use at the stations. Set up six stations (card tables, etc.) labeled: *Church, Giving, Missions, Witnessing, Studying the Bible,* and *Helping Others.* At each station, have a list of choices for that station and the chip exchanges that go with each choice (see pp. 48–49), extra chips, and paper for "receipts." Also, recruit six attendants (one for each station).

Scripture: Joshua 1:8; Jeremiah 9:23–24; Matthew 28:19–20; 2 Corinthians 9:6–7; Galatians 6:9–10; Hebrews 10:24–25; 1 Peter 3:15

The Exercise:

The leader gives each participant an envelope containing the chips (as above). Leader emphasizes that this envelope contains all the student has ever dreamed of in terms of money, ability, time, and popularity. Congratulate them for having "made it." Students have twenty minutes to visit the six stations in the room and collect, trade, or spend their chips as they desire. At each booth is a three-question survey. After the students tell the attendant their answers to the survey

· ·

questions, the attendant exchanges chips with them and gives them a card that records the choices they made.

When time is up, call the students back together and divide them up into groups of four to answer discussion questions and study Bible verses for each of the six topics.

Discussion Questions:
1. Why did you choose the things you did? How do you feel about your choices?
2. What does the Bible say God wants us to choose? Look up the following verses for some hints. Write your answer in the space next to the verse.
   a) Church
      Hebrews 10:24–25
   b) Giving
      2 Corinthians 9:6–7
   c) Missions
      Matthew 28:19–20
   d) Witnessing
      1 Peter 3:15
   e) Studying the Bible
      Joshua 1:8
   f) Helping Others
      Galatians 6:9–10

Summary and Conclusion:
To conclude the session, the leader summarizes what the Bible says about each choice and points out that having less in worldly chips means you are living more in accord with God's desires. Read Matthew 6:19–20 and Jeremiah 9:23–24 to the group.

Finally, each participant takes several minutes to write a personal application of the lesson. What are you going to do about choosing what God wants? It may help to complete the following statement: This week I will spend my chips for God by:

Where Your Heart Is

Booths and Choices

Your Choices	Your Chips

CHURCH

1. You almost always go to church on Sunday mornings and Wednesday nights because you really like it. — Give 2 time chips

2. You spend Wednesday nights and Sundays with your family and friends doing things other than going to church. — Get 2 popularity chips

3. You usually have to work or study Sundays and Wednesday nights. — Get 2 ability chips / 2 money chips

GIVING

1. You put 10% of your allowance and the money you earn in the offering plate at church. — Give 2 money chips

2. You put a lot of your money in a savings account at the bank. — Get 2 money chips

3. You spend most of your money on your friends, having fun, or buying things that you want. — Get 2 popularity chips / 1 money chip

MISSIONS

1. You go on a missions trip to Mexico over spring break to help kids in an orphanage. — Give 1 time chip / Give 1 ability chip / Give 1 money chip

2. You read the newspaper so you will know what is happening in the world. — Get 2 ability chips

3. Whenever you hear there is going to be something about missions, you try to find something else to do because missionaries are so boring. — Get 1 time chip / 1 popularity chip

WITNESSING

1. You like to tell others about becoming a Christian and you do so every chance you get.

   Give 1 time chip
       2 popularity chips

2. Your friends know you are a Christian, but you don't talk about it much because you don't want to turn them off.

   Get 1 popularity chip

3. You usually forget to talk about Christ because other things are on your mind.

   Get 2 time chips
       1 ability chip

STUDYING THE BIBLE

1. You study the Bible almost every day because you want to know what God says you should do.

   Give 1 time chip
       1 popularity chip
       1 ability chip

2. You don't like to study the Bible because it's so hard to understand.

   Get 1 time chip

3. You hardly ever have time because you're so busy working, being with your friends, taking lessons, or doing other things.

   Get 1 time chip
       1 ability chip
       1 popularity chip
       1 money chip

HELPING OTHERS

1. You help every time you see there are things you can do.

   Give 2 money chips
       1 time chip
       1 ability chip

2. You would help people who are cool, if their car broke down or something like that.

   Get 2 popularity chips

3. You think it's better not to get involved because people might begin to expect too much.

   Get 2 money chips
       1 time chip
       1 ability chip

Exercise Ten

. . . .

My Coat of Arms

by Mervin Birky

Age: Youth (also adaptable to Adult Small Groups)

Setting: A group of 10–30 persons. Definitely NOT an icebreaker! This exercise will increase intimacy in a group which already feels somewhat comfortable being together.

Time: About 30 minutes

Goal: To increase the value participants place upon their worth as unique products of God's creativity.

Leader Preparation: Pieces of construction paper cut out and marked like a blank coat of arms (see illustration p. 52); one blank coat of arms, a pen, and a safety pin for each participant (Or, make one photocopy of the coat of arms page for each participant); a watch with a second hand, and a Bible

Scripture: Psalm 139:1–6, 13–16; Matthew 5:2; Luke 12:6–7; 1 Corinthians 15:10a

The Exercise:
A. Give each person the blank coat of arms, a pen, and a safety pin.
   1. On the board, draw a large blank coat of arms and instructions about how to fill it out, using the sample coat of arms (p. 52).
   2. It's important for the leader(s) to do a coat of arms, too.
B. When all participants have filled out a coat of arms, they should pin it to their shirts/blouses just below their chins. Then do the following:
   1. Have students count off by twos and then form two concentric circles facing each other. When the timekeeper calls "Time," the outer circle will move one person to the right while the inner circle stays in place. In this way, every person will eventually have an opportunity to interact with everyone in the other circle.

. . . .

Building Biblical Values

2. Tell students to maintain complete silence. No talking, joking, whispering, etc.
3. When the timekeeper calls "Go," have the pairs read the information on each others' coat of arms and look directly into each others' eyes for 10–15 seconds.
4. Timekeeper will call "Switch" every 20–30 seconds (depending upon how rapidly this group can read). At this signal move to the next person and read their card, etc.
5. When the outer circle has made a complete rotation, call "Stop."

Summary and Conclusion:
Questions for quiet meditation (As the leader, you know your group and whether they should quietly listen to these questions or use them for open discussion):
1. What things on your coat of arms were you most happy to let others see? What things (if any) were you embarrassed to have others see?
2. What things might you change if you were to redo this exercise right now?
3. Read Psalm 139:1–6 and 13–16 slowly to the group from a modern translation and say, "By doing this exercise you have allowed these other people to learn some things about you today. Would any of these things be a surprise to God?"
4. Do you feel differently about some of what you wrote now that you see what other people have written? Which items?
5. Were there some answers you saw that you thought were especially interesting or about which you wanted to ask questions? Which ones?
6. Were there some persons you felt more comfortable with than others? Why do you think this was so?
7. How has this exercise affected the way you feel about yourself?

My Coat of Arms*

Name: _____

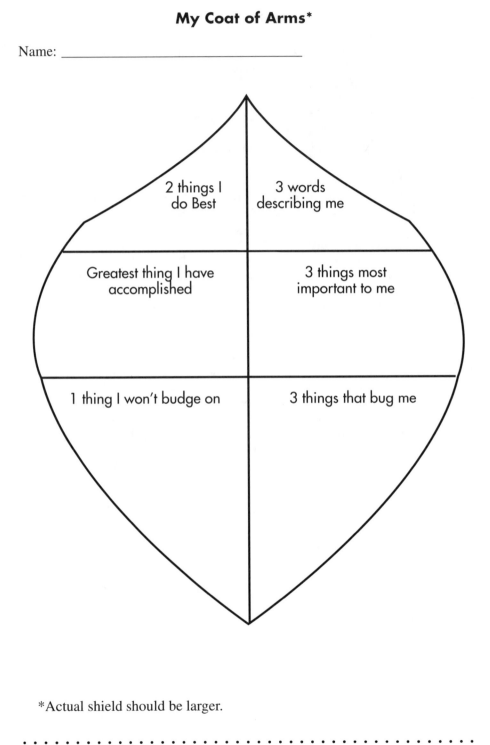

2 things I do Best

3 words describing me

Greatest thing I have accomplished

3 things most important to me

1 thing I won't budge on

3 things that bug me

*Actual shield should be larger.

Apply Empathy to a Dilemma

Age: Junior High

Setting: Group

Time: 45 minutes

Goal: In the setting of a moral dilemma, to provide an opportunity for youth to exercise empathy and apply the Scripture to a hypothetical case and to each person's life

Leader Preparation: Paper, pencils, and a chalkboard

Scripture: Matthew 7:12

The Exercise:
Students will play out an improvised skit with the following characters and scenario:

Characters: Elwood, the Oddball
David, Joe-average Christian
Remington, the All-Star

Scenario: David is your average Christian junior higher, just trying to maintain himself. Lately, he's been a little concerned about Elwood, who is generally left out of everything. On Thursday, Elwood (much to David's surprise) asked Dave if he would come over to his house on Saturday and watch a bunch of sci-fi films on his VCR. David agreed. Then on Friday night, Remington Clark, Mister All-Everything who everybody wants to chum up to, phones Dave and invites him to come to his birthday party at Glenwood Springs—all expenses paid. And when is this wonderful party going to be? You guessed it: Saturday!

What should Dave do?

Discussion:

1. Ask the students: What would *you* do? Everybody, write your answers on a piece of paper and turn them in. *Leader:* Write these answers, plus any other options the class can think of, on the board.

2. Introduce the Scripture (Matthew 7:12) and talk about it. Emphasize that what we do has an important effect on other people, and not just on the nice people.

3. Have students pair up and finish these sentences: "One time when somebody made me feel really crummy, even though he/she wasn't trying to, he/she . . ." and "One time when somebody did something that made me feel just great, he/she . . ."

4. Have the class brainstorm the feelings Elwood and Remington would probably have about each option listed on the board. Write the feelings next to each option.

5. Divide the class into groups of four and have each group choose the "right" option on the basis of Scripture and discuss the impact on the people involved. Have each group share its answer with the larger group and justify it with reasons. After each group has spoken, see if the entire class can reach a group consensus.

Summary and Conclusion:

1. Have the class pair up again. Each person should think of "somebody you know who is hurting and could really use a 'Do unto' this week."

2. Tell your partner and pray with each other about your situations.

3. Exchange phone numbers and agree to check in with each other this week to see how things are working out.

Peter and Patient Obedience

by Wayne Blanchard

Age: Junior High through High School

Setting: Group

Time: 20 minutes

Goal: To allow youth to experience a situation where patience is valuable to deal with authority, thus encouraging them to prize the trait of patience and to empathize with the challenges authorities face in leading and instructing them when they are not patient

Leader Preparation: Pens, a Bible, and copies of the Sunday School Class Quiz (p. 56) for all participants

Scripture: Hebrews 6:12

The Exercise:
1. Pass out the Sunday School Class Quiz (p. 56), face down, to the students.
2. Explain that they have ten minutes to complete the sheet.
3. All answers must be in ink, and no one can scratch out an answer once it has been written.
4. Instruct the students to turn the sheet over and begin.

Summary and Conclusion:
1. Ask, "Who read all of the instructions before answering? Who did not?" Let this part be lighthearted and humorous.
2. To those who began to fill out the sheet:

a) How did you feel when you read question 7?
b) Were the directions at the top of the sheet clear?
c) Did you understand the directions when you read them?
d) What were some of your reasons for jumping in and answering before reading the directions?

3. To the entire group:
a) Are there times when your parents give you clear instructions before you do something?
b) Do you ever feel you can do it better your own way?
c) In what sorts of situations would you rather do it your own way?
d) Give some examples. (These may be serious or humorous. The leaders should give personal examples from their own lives, if possible.)
e) How do you react?
f) Are you always pleased with the results?
g) If not, what is a better solution?
h) If you really do have a better way of doing the activity, what is the best way to work it out?

Sunday School Class Quiz

Directions: Follow these instructions carefully. Read 1 Peter 3:13–20. After carefully reading this passage, read all the questions before answering.

1. How does Peter describe those who suffer for righteousnes' sake?

2. When people want to know the reason for our hope and peace, with what should we be ready?

3. How is this answer to be given?

4. What will happen to those evildoers who falsely accuse our good Christian behavior?

5. When Peter is speaking of suffering righteously, who comes to his mind?

6. What is the difference between Christ's sufferings at human hands and any suffering we may be called upon to endure?

7. Skip questions 1 through 6 and write only your name on this paper.

Capturing Time

by J'Anne Stuckey

Age: Junior High through College

Setting: Class or group

Time: 30 minutes

Goal: To provide students with an opportunity to examine how they use their time and to reflect upon the value they place on fellowship (time alone) with God

Leader Preparation: A copy of the Time Survey chart (p. 58) for each student and pencils; a blackboard and a couple of pocket calculators also helpful

Scripture: Ecclesiastes 12:1a; Ephesians 5:15–17

The Exercise:
1. Begin by passing out the Time Survey (p. 58) and have students fill it out.
2. While they are filling it out, put a copy of the survey on the board.
3. When students have completed their surveys, use the board to show approximate amounts of time the "average" student spends on priority activities.
4. As a group, discuss these activities, including how they became priorities. Was this a deliberate choice or just a result of circumstances? Are they pleased with the pattern of how they use their time, or is time simply getting away from them?

Summary and Conclusion:
As a group, address the issue of time alone with God.
1. How would you change the way you use your time for God?
2. What is the best (most practical, realistic, and workable) way to set up a devotional time?

Time Survey

Assume that you have a sixteen-hour day. With that in mind, fill in the following chart, indicating as accurately as possible how you spend your time on an average day. Do not include weekends or holidays.

Activity	Hours/Minutes
Classes	_____
Sports	_____
Telephoning	_____
With friends	_____
Watching TV	_____
Work	_____
Chores	_____
Studying	_____
Meals/snacks	_____
Clubs	_____
Bible study, devotions	_____
Other activities not listed above	_____

Total Hours: 16

Answer these questions by studying the above chart:

1. I spend most of my time doing _____.

2. I like the way I spend my time.   Yes   No

3. From this chart, I can see that my major priority right now is _____.

4. My second major priority is _____.

5. Looking at the week just past, I spent _____ hours (total) alone with God (personal devotion time away from other people).

Who's My Boss

by Linda Haymond

Age: Junior High through College

Setting: Individual or group

Time: 20 minutes

Goal: To evaluate the attitudes we hold about our work

Leader Preparation: One Attitude and Behavior Chart (p. 60), a Bible, and a pencil for each individual

Scripture: Romans 12:17; 13:13; Philippians 4:8; Colossians 3:23; Hebrews 13:18

The Exercise:
1. With a job comes lots of responsibility. On the job we are often in positions where our values are challenged. If our behavior contradicts a value that we hold, it causes some real conflicts inside us. But we also need to examine how our contradictory actions affect others such as our families and the companies we work for.
2. Complete the Attitude and Behavior Chart (p. 60).

Summary and Conclusion:
After participants have completed the chart, discuss the following questions:
1. Should my responses to these situations be governed by God, myself, my family, or my company?
2. What does the Bible say about honesty in our work? Look up each verse and briefly summarize it in your own words. Can you identify a conclusion from all the verses taken together?

Attitude and Behavior Chart

Directions: Before each statement write an **N** if it would not concern you, a **P** if it would concern you personally, an **F** if it would concern your family, and a **C** if it would concern your company. You may use more than 1 letter before each statement. These sample incidents may not involve you personally at this time, but answer as though you were involved.

Responses	**Statement**

1.   There is a lot of food left over in the company's dining room. No one is around, so you help yourself without paying for the items.

2.   There are certain materials that companies use for advertisements. Often I take home gum, pencils, and pens.

3.   You are a salesperson who is often on the road. Because of this responsibility, you have a generous expense account. You turned in a voucher that went slightly over your actual expenses.

4.   Because you travel in the company car, you have a company credit card for fuel. Occasionally you have used this credit card for fuel in your own car.

5.   Insurance restricts the use of the company car to employees only. This means family members are excluded, but they use the car frequently anyway.

Deceptive Packaging

by Alan Knott

Age: Junior High through College

Setting: Group

Time: 15–20 minutes

Goal: To stimulate youth (1) to consider and become aware of their values about people and whether they judge them by appearance or intrinsic value as beings created in the image of God; (2) to be exposed to what the Bible says concerning judging; (3) to evaluate their actions and values in the light of Scripture; (4) to act upon their present values concerning people, using an exercise; (5) to discuss the reasons for their decisions; (6) to respond to the Bible's values (The rationale is to create a situation of cognitive disequilibrium and appeal to stage 3 (focus on interpersonal relations seeking reciprocity), stage 4 (maintenance of social order with fixed rules and authority), the student's ability to put self in another's shoes, and the student's sense of fairness and equality. (See appendix 1 for Kohlberg's stages.)

Leader Preparation: Four dimes for each participant, items of various values including $5 hidden in an old paper bag

Scripture: Luke 6:37–38; James 2:1–13

The Exercise:
1. Give each student four dimes.
2. On the floor (or on a table) spread out items of various worth.
3. Among the items include a crumpled up old paper bag. Without the students being aware of it, you have put a $5 bill in this bag.
4. Invite the students to use their dimes to bid for the items spread out.
5. They can keep the item they bid for but cannot bid any more after they have obtained one item.

Summary and Conclusion:
There are two possible outcomes:

1. *One person bids and gets the paper bag.* Have this person open it and look inside. Affirm the person and then ask the person to explain why he or she bid for the paper bag. Ask the others why they did not bid for it. Lead them to the Scriptures, and discuss that we should not judge people by appearance but consider all people as being of great value because they are made in the image of God. Emphasize that the package does not always give away what is inside.

2. *No one bids for the paper bag.* When bidding is complete, you pick the bag up and show the group the $5 bill that was in it. Have the class discuss why they did not bid for an old paper bag. Ask them if this is not the way we sometimes treat people who may not be well-groomed, may not wear the right brands of clothes, may not be in the in crowd, may not have a cool haircut, may come from poverty—in other words, an outsider. Using the Luke passage, point out the blessings Jesus says come with judging people mercifully. Also examine the James passage.

Exercise Sixteen

. . . .

Saint Elsewhere

Age: Youth, ages 14–16

Setting: Group

Time: About 60 minutes

Goal: To learn to value judging others as God judges

. . . .

Building Biblical Values

Leader Preparation: Select 4 people ahead of time to be patients; blackboard or poster, Bibles, and copies of the Prayer of St. Francis of Assisi

Scripture: Matthew 7:1–5; Romans 14:10; 1 Corinthians 2:12–15; Philippians 1:9–10

The Exercise:
    A. Choose 4 members and isolate them from the group, explaining the strategy of the exercise.
    B. Have the group sit down in a semicircle, facing one direction. Explain to the group that they will be asked to assume the role of members of a special medical panel that will make a crucial decision affecting the lives of 4 persons and their families and loved ones.

[Bring the 4 patients in and have them sit quietly while the medical director presents the cases.]

Dr. Williams: Hello, I'm Dr. Henry Williams. Today you've been called together to consider 4 patients who need the help of our therapy machine, which could save their lives. Unfortunately, we have only one machine, so we can treat only one patient. First, let's examine the case histories. Then we'll discuss each patient and decide which 1 should receive the therapy.
    1. Our first case is Melissa Barrow, who is thirty-two years old. Melissa works at home as a typist so she can earn extra money and still be with her children. She and her husband have two children, Billy, nine, and Linda, six. Billy and Linda depend on their mother and her constant attention. They don't see too much of their father because he's a salesperson and frequently away from home. Mrs. Barrow tries to do an many things as she can with her children and give them as much care as possible. Certainly, if anything happened to Melissa, it would be a tremendous loss to her family.
    2. Our second applicant is Dr. Roland Barton, who will be forty-eight in a couple of days. Dr. Barton is married with no children. He's been highly acclaimed in the past for his medical research work, and he's presently trying to discover a cure for leukemia. Dr. Barton also teaches a seminar two days a week at the University Medical School. He has taught there for almost a decade and during that time has been instrumental in training many successful doctors.
    3. Our third case history belongs to Terry Leland. All we can say about Terry is that he enjoys many of the same activities as other seven-year-old boys. Terry is delightful—intelligent, active, full of life. He might have a very promising future if he could get the treatment he needs to live.
    4. Finally, there's Walter Fredericks, twenty-seven, a civic leader

who's devoted himself to the problems facing blacks who live in the city. Mr. Fredericks has been chiefly concerned with improving existing housing conditions, ending discrimination in hiring practices, and reducing unemployment. Mr. Fredericks also seems committed to young people. He understands their feelings and tries to encourage their ideas. In fact, Mr. Fredericks was just recently appointed special assistant to the mayor for youth activities. Needless to say, there are many new programs he hopes to develop over the coming years.

[Allow the patients to leave the room.]

Dr. Williams: Well, you've met four very different people. Of course we can treat only one of them, so let's decide which person should be given the help we have to offer.

C. Ask for a vote on which patient is to receive the therapy machine. Allow *no discussion.*

   Tabulate the votes. Take the results out of the room and share them with the patients. Give them a few moments to collect their thoughts.

[All the patients rejoin the group, sitting quietly.]

D. Each of the four patients has three minutes to explain to the group why he or she should be reconsidered for therapy. Allow the patients to make very strong (positive or negative) religious statements in their explanations.

[After each patient has made a presentation, thank them all and allow them to leave the room.]

E. Vote again. *No discussion.*

[Invite the persons acting as patients to join the group and to drop their roles.]

Summary and Conclusion:
1. Why did we vote as we did the first time? What did we notice that caused us to choose this individual?
2. Why did we vote as we did the second time? What insights from the additional information caused us to choose this individual?
3. Open discussion: Are we as Christian young people called to judge?
    a) What are we *not* to judge?
    b) What *are* we to judge?

4. Break into small groups. Have each group take a passage from Scripture and summarize what it says about principles regarding human judgment. Take notes to report back to the large group.
   a) Matthew 7:1–5 (begin with self-judgment)
   b) 1 Corinthians 2:12–15 (become spiritually minded)
   c) Philippians 1:9–10 (abound in love)
   d) Romans 14:10 (await the final judgment)
5. Report back to the large group. Allow time for discussion.

Close with a group recitation (use a transparency or make copies) of the Prayer of St. Francis of Assisi.

. . . .

Johari's Window, Revised

by Sue Kruter Grayson

Age: High School through Adult

Setting: Best with a cohesive group where all participants know each other

Time: About 60 minutes

Goal: To focus on self-image, comparing and contrasting how participants view themselves, are viewed by each other, and how God views them; to stimulate participants to value God's image of them as the most important and most valid, appreciating the fact that it is based upon God's grace and not human traits (Students will move through Raths, Harmin, and Simon's step 6, acting upon choices)

. . . .

Leader Preparation: Two papers and pencils for each participant; you can draw the window panes on the board for them to copy, or you can hand out ready-made windows on paper that you have prepared; Bibles, concordance for reference, and a board to list students' suggestions

Scripture: Psalm 139

The Exercise:
  A. Johari's Window is a tool to compare differing views of the self. The "window" on the paper will have four "panes."
  B. Use the two panes on the left as the first two panes. In the top left, write how you see yourself. In the bottom left pane, write how you think others see you. Do this for yourself. This is not for others to see. (Allow 8–10 minutes for this step.)
  C. If it will help organize their thinking, you can give participants an outline of items to consider: strengths and weaknesses in the areas of the physical, emotional, mental, spiritual, etc.
  D. Now, the third pane is how someone else sees you. Using the spare sheet of paper provided, cover up the windowpanes on the left. Pair up and write in the third box how you see each other. (Allow 5–7 minutes.)
  E. Discussion:
Let's talk about these three panes so far.
  1. Were there differences between how you viewed yourself and how you thought others viewed you? What causes these differences? Is it proper that there are differences? Why or why not?
  2. Were there differences in how you thought someone else would view you and how he or she actually did? Why or why not? To decide what you think and how you feel about yourself, whose viewpoint should count the most, yours or others'? Why?
  3. What would provide the most accurate view of who you really are?
  4. What should you put in the fourth pane? Fill it with God's image of you.
  5. What *is* God's image of you? What Scriptures apply here? Who can think of some? (Write these down on the board as they come for everyone to see. Encourage use of the concordance, if needed. If students can't think of any Scriptures, direct them to Psalm 139 to prime the pump.)
  6. Using this information, fill in the fourth pane, making the information personal.
  7. Knowing what you've put in the fourth pane, how does that affect you? Does it alter what you have in the first pane? How might this view of yourself change your feelings and behavior?
  8. Does how people feel about themselves affect their behavior? Give some examples. (The movie *Free Willy* contains an example of this.)

Are there any examples in Scripture of people's actions changing because they know how God sees them?

9. How could this idea of self-image affecting behavior change your life?

Summary and Conclusion:

When you get home, fill in the first pane again in view of God's image of you. Thank God for His great grace. Make a list of feelings and behaviors you want God to change in you. Ask Him to do this transforming work within you, and promise to cooperate. Make it a practice to continue to focus on His positive image of you based upon His grace (Romans 12:1–2).

Exercise Eighteen

· ·

The Values Auction

Adapted from *Success* magazine

Age: High School through Adult

Setting: Group

Time: 30–60 minutes

Goal: To help people consider using their resources to secure life's greatest possessions

Leader Preparation: Play money from a board game or "money" you make; cut-up small pieces of paper for receipts; other props; recruit an auctioneer; a list of "valuables" appropriate for your group; several leading questions and humorous remarks; a large board or poster and a Bible for reference

Scripture: Matthew 6:19–21, 16:26

· ·

The Exercise:

Introduction: Do not relate what you say directly to the values auction. Make your remarks sound like an off-the-cuff discussion. Start by talking about Christ's eye-of-a-needle analogy. Or begin the session with a question: Does anybody know what a value is? What is materialism? Do people ever say one thing and do the exact opposite? Prepare a series of leading questions to use later. These questions should highlight both the exercise and the Christian concepts you are teaching.

Instructions for the Auction: Give each participant several thousand dollars to spend. Put up the list of items where everyone can see it, and let the participants go over the list before bidding begins. Otherwise, some will run out of money before they can bid on what they really want.

This auction will be the most fun if you have a bookkeeper who takes participants' money and gives them a receipt and a real auctioneer to run the auction. The leader can mark the names of who bought what on the list on the board.

The Auction: Have bidding begin on the first item. Depending on how the bidding goes, 1 participant may or may not be able to purchase more than one item. Keep the atmosphere lighthearted. If you can't locate a real auctioneer, then mix in lots of jokes and good humor yourself.

Make sure your list of valuables matches the age group and that they really are valuable in the eyes of this particular group. For example, popularity with the in-group is probably more important to adolescents than adults. Here is a list of possible valuables from which to choose.

- A brand new home
- Having close friends for life
- A new car every year for life
- A certificate good for one answered prayer
- Good health for life
- A cure for cancer
- Superior athletic ability
- Guaranteed good looks
- Heaven assured
- Worldwide fame in your career
- Every member of your family a Christian
- God's approval on your life's work
- Dinner for two at the best restaurant in town
- Large Bible commentary set
- Ten gift certificates for dinner for two at the best restaurant in town
- Satisfying, effective daily prayer life
- Your own apartment for three years
- Unlimited meals at McDonald's for three years
- Knowing God better

- Going on a thirty-day ocean cruise
- Making all As in school
- New car
- Having a church to go to
- Having many Christian friends

Summary and Conclusion:

When the auction is over, the most crucial part begins: the follow-up discussion. You want the discussion to make a lasting impression. Here it is important not to preach or to supply ready-made answers but to ask insight-producing questions (see appendixes 3 and 5). Components you could include:

1. Specific instances of bidding that came up during the auction
2. Tying in some of your original set of questions from the introduction
3. Bible passages that relate to the values in the auction

. . . .

Animal Representations

Age: Youth through Adult

Setting: Groups that need to become better acquainted; team building

Time: 15–30 minutes (depends upon size of group)

Goal: To reinforce character strengths of each participant and make each aware of his or her personality traits that need more development; a caring group will start to work and pray with each person in a new way as a result of this exercise

Leader Preparation: Paper and pen for each participant; a stimulating introduction

Scripture: Romans 12; 1 Corinthians 12:12–27

The Exercise:

Ask each person to write on a piece of paper the name of an animal that best depicts the character of each person in the group including himself or herself.

Here are some examples to get you started: owls for their wisdom or their quiet observation, cocker spaniels for their friskiness, Labrador retrievers for their calm intelligence, monkeys for their activity and love of fun, foxes for their cunning. You may want to refer to a resource such as Bill Gothard's *Character Sketches* from the Institute for Basic Youth Conflicts for further suggestions. (The Bible also has some observations about animals, such as the prudent ant.)

Summary and Conclusion:

Ask participants to talk about the animals they chose and the reasons why. It will be fascinating to see how close others' representation of you match your own.

Finish up by reading "A Rabbit on the Swim Team" from Chuck Swindoll's *Home: Where Life Makes Up Its Mind* (Multnomah Press, 1979, p. 51).

. . . .

A Bite at a Time

Used by permission from G/L Publishers, Glendale CA 91209

Age: Youth through Adult

Setting: Group or one-to-one discipleship

Time: 45–60 minutes

Goal: To make the participants more conscious of how they use their time and to help them set goals to better use their time

Leader Preparation: A copy of Schedules for Student A and Student B (p. 73) and Discussion Questions (p. 72) for each participant. For additional help, see chapter 12 of *How to Decide What's Really Important* by Fritz Ridenour (Ventura, Calif.: Regal Books, 1978)

Scripture: Ephesians 5:15–17

The Exercise:
   A.   Read the Scripture and the following poem. How do they connect?

> Lord, help me to laugh and smile,
>   not because I have to
>   but because I love You.
> Help me to love people,
>   not because it's my duty
>   but because You love them.
> Help me to love them
>   for what they are
>   where they are.
> Give me confidence
>   to trust people
>   and believe in them.

Give me the stamina
   to share myself with them
   and to give all of myself to You.
Give me the nerve to ask for Your directions,
   then make me a bonfire
   with Your love the flame.

—Author Unknown

B. Sometimes the tasks we need to do seem huge and overwhelming. Here is a riddle to answer: How do you eat an elephant?*

C. Study the chart on page 73. This chart gives a record of how two different students (student A and student B) spent their time during the school week. Then, answer the discussion questions listed below.

D. Now, create a sample plan for periods of one year, one month, one week, and one day, that would help you in your own life:
1. develop closer Christian friendships
2. be a more appealing "walking commercial" for the Christian faith
3. be more kind or helpful at home
4. (Write you own personal goal)
For example:
> One-year goal: Read one-third of the Bible, taking notes on God's traits
> One-month goal: Read one book of the Bible
> One-week goal: Read three chapters of the Bible
> One-day goal: Read daily

Summary and Conclusion:

Ask God to show you one area to improve your use of time for Him and make a schedule for it. Post the schedule where you can see it every day. In partnership with God, figure out a "reward" for meeting your goal. Commit to the goal and pray that God will give you the power to reach it.

* Answer: A bite at a time.

Discussion Questions

1. What would you say are student A's and student B's values?
2. Both students feel a need to redeem the time and spend 15 minutes a day in Bible reading and prayer. Suggest three ways each student could do that.
3. These students want closer Christian friendships with young people from church. How could each arrange his or her schedule to allow for that?
4. What would be the cost for each student to make the above changes— that is, what are some of the possible consequences or results?

Schedules for Student A and Student B

	MON	TUE	WED	THU	FRI
6:00–7:30	GET UP, HAVE BREAKFAST, CATCH BUS				
8:00–12:00	**A** Classes	Study Hall	Classes	Study Hall	Classes
	B Classes	Classes	Classes	Classes	3 Classes 1 Study Hall
12:00–12:30	LUNCH				
12:30–3:00	**A** 1 Class 2 Study Halls	Classes	Classes	Classes	1 Class often cut
	B 2 Classes 1 Study Hall	Classes	Classes	Classes	2 Classes 1 Study Hall
3:00–5:00	**A** Cokes with friends	Guitar lesson	Soap opera on TV	Watch team work out on athletic field	Cokes with friends
	B Sports practice	Practice	Game	Practice	Practice
5:00–6:00	DINNER AND CHORES AT HOME				
6:00–10:00	**A** TV, some homework	TV all evening	Two hours on phone, TV	Phone, half-hour homework	Downtown with friends
	B Homework and TV	Homework and TV	Homework and TV	Meeting to plan team banquet	Downtown with team and their dates
10:00–11:00	**A** Reading magazines	Late show	On phone	On phone	TV
	B Reading *Sports Illustrated*	On phone	Already in bed	On phone with current date	TV

Exercise Twenty-One
· ·

The Evangelism Game

by D. Yngsdal

Age: Youth through Adult

Setting: Group (40 or more) with adequate space to move around (preferably a gym or fellowship hall, etc.)

Time: 40–60 minutes

Goal: To assist participants to see the value of becoming personally involved with evangelism, to give participants opportunities to repeat the facts of the Gospel, and as a potential outreach event for unsaved friends

Leader Preparation: Large posters labeled "Heaven" and "Hell"; tapes or CDs of scary music, like the theme from *Jaws,* and quiet music for in between; copies of The Gospel (see p. 77); a list of ways to die for the announcer to use. Prepare an announcer and some counselors in advance with a thorough understanding of the rules of the game so they can coach the participants. *Additional options:* Since the key to this game is a playful spirit, props to make the game more exciting could include dry ice to make "smoke" going up from hell, haloes for saints as they enter heaven, cardboard flames for hell and clouds, gold bricks or a rainbow for heaven. Be creative!

Scripture: John 3:16; 10:10; 14:6; Romans 3:23; 5:8, 23; Ephesians 2:8–9

The Exercise:
1. Designate and label two areas on opposite sides of the large room, one as heaven, and one as hell.
2. Have the announcer prepared with a script of ways to die and the music you have chosen. (Ways to die: floods, earthquakes, fires, etc.)
3. Designate two or three people to be counselors, and point out where they are stationed.

· ·

4. Divide participants into groups of about ten each, and scatter the groups around the room. Ask folks in each group to count off, so that each group member is numbered from 1 to 10 (or however many there are in that group).
5. Choose one person who is "saved." Give this person a copy of "The Gospel." When the announcer says, "Go!" the saved person must go to someone in any group and get that person to respond to "The Gospel."
6. When the "lost" person can repeat "The Gospel" to the saved person, the saved person takes the lost person to a counselor. Here, the lost person must repeat "The Gospel" to the counselor. Once this is done accurately, the lost person is now considered "saved," for purposes of the game, and is commissioned by the counselor to go and tell others "The Gospel."
7. During this time, while the lost are becoming saved, the announcer will interrupt the background music from time to time and play the scary music, call for attention, and announce that people with a certain number have just died.
8. Those whose "number is up" must immediately report either to heaven or hell, depending on whether or not they've had a chance to hear and respond to "The Gospel."
9. The game is over when all the people have died and are either in heaven or hell.
10. Here is an example of how the game operates. After the rules are explained and the announcer says "Go," the one saved person starts out to witness. After he or she has reached a few people and they've gone to the counselor, the announcer plays the scary music and says, "May I have your attention." At this, all activity is suspended and the announcer continues, "A 747 has crashed and all the number 5s have just died. Please report to your designated areas." Those who have completed the process of repeating "The Gospel" to a counselor are saved and may go to heaven. All those who have not yet responded to "The Gospel" must go to hell. Then, the game resumes.

A person can only respond to "The Gospel" if a "saved" person witnesses to him or her. If a person who is brought to a counselor is unable to repeat "The Gospel" to the counselor, he or she is still "lost," must return to his or her group and await another witness. If a person is hearing "The Gospel" when the announcer announces his or her death, the person is still lost and must go to hell. If a person is repeating "The Gospel" to a counselor when his or her number is called, that person may go to heaven if able to complete the recitation without any errors.

Instruct those who go to heaven that they should rejoice. Remind them to rejoice as they notice people responding to "The Gospel," and as the saved people die and join them in heaven. (Let them whoop it up!) Those who land in hell should quietly watch the people in heaven.

From the beginning, it is important to emphasize to players that this is only a game representing the evangelism process. The game contains many symbols. For example, when the lost person repeats "The Gospel" to the witness, it represents having "head knowledge" of "The Gospel." When lost persons repeat "The Gospel" to the counselor, this represents their asking Christ to be their Lord and Savior.

Summary and Conclusion:

It is essential to the effectiveness of this exercise to have everyone come together for the discussion time at the end. Here are some questions to spark discussion.

1. What were some frustrations?

2. To those who went to hell, "Why weren't you told?" Did the witnesses go to their friends first?

3. Was it hard to remember the facts of "The Gospel?"

4. How did you feel about going up to the "lost" and reciting "The Gospel" to them? Was it easier or harder than you anticipated?

5. Did you think it was fair? (You had to be reached by a witness before you could be saved even if you wanted to be saved.)

6. How did it feel to die?

7. How did those in hell feel, looking at those in heaven?

8. How did those in heaven feel? When you looked into hell, were there people there you knew?

9. By the time the game was over, how many people ended up going to heaven as the result of a chain of response to one "saved" person who was willing to share the "Gospel"?

10. What else can we learn from this game? How well does it line up with the truth of salvation from the Bible?

11. How many people would *really* like to get saved right now?

To sum up the total experience in a moment of commitment, play a song like "Send Us to the World" by Harvest or "Give Me the Words" by Farell and Farell.

The Gospel

1. God loves you and offers a wonderful plan for your life.

   A. John 3:16

   B. John 10:10

2. Every person is sinful and separated from God. Therefore we cannot know and experience God's love and plan for our lives.

   A. Romans 3:23

   B. Romans 6:23

3. Jesus is God's only provision for our sin. Through Him we can know and experience God's love and plan for our lives.

   A. Romans 5:8

   B. John 14:6

4. We must individually receive Jesus as Savior and Lord. Then we can know and experience God's love and plan for our lives.

   A. John 1:12

   B. Ephesians 2:8–9

Exercise Twenty-Two

Getting to Know You

by Becky McKenna

Age: Youth through Adult

Setting: Groups of 15–30 people that need encouragement to get acquainted, such as leadership groups, women's groups, couples' groups, and groups that would benefit from relating on a deeper level

Time: 45 minutes (may vary)

Goal: To promote openness, especially among members of a group or among friends

Leader Preparation: A large piece of plain paper for each person; a variety of magazines: news, auto, sports, women's, baby care, music groups, and some Christian magazines; scissors; markers; glue; a poster with the following questions to guide interviews:

1. Why is this picture (word, drawing) important to you?
2. What does this say about you as a person?
3. How does this fit in with God's plan for you?

Scripture: 1 Corinthians 12:12, 25

The Exercise:
1. Give each person all of the supplies listed above to work with, but keep the poster hidden away. Ask each to make a collage including pictures, drawings, or words that will give a picture of who he or she is. Allow freedom for creativity. If some people need specific guidelines, it may be helpful to suggest that they include people who are important in their lives, principles they believe in, or areas they are talented in. Be sure they are aware of the time limit (20 minutes).
2. After all finish, ask each to find a partner. Stress that it should be someone

he or she wants to get to know better, not a close friend. Leader should assist those who are hesitant (stragglers) to find partners. Have the pairs discuss the collages in an interview form, following the questions on the poster you now display. One person asks questions about the other's collage. Halfway through the exercise, call time and have partners switch who interviews. Open-ended questions besides the ones on the poster may be added (20 minutes).

Summary and Conclusion:
Have someone read the Scripture out loud. Discuss the value of transparency in reference to Jesus' life and God's will. Have a group cleanup time (5 minutes).

Exercise Twenty-Three

The Great Giver

by Harold Westing

Age: Junior High

Setting: Group

Time: 45–90 minutes (depends upon size of group)

Goal: To learn to value giving things away rather than keeping things for oneself

Leader Preparation: The list of items to rank written on a chart, blackboard, or on handouts for individuals to study; paper and pencils and a Bible available

Scripture: Matthew 6:21

The Exercise:
A. Please rate the following items according to how important they are to you. Put the most valuable first and the least valuable last.
   - New car
   - Girlfriend or boyfriend
   - Happy home
   - Knowing God has accepted you as a Christian
   - Snowmobile or motorcycle
   - Wholesome Christian friends
   - Being free from guilt
   - Feeling very happy
   - Spending an hour with God in prayer and Bible study
B. Questions for group discussion:
   1. Tell the group why you put these in the order you did. Back up your decision with sound reasoning.
   2. How do you decide if something is valuable? (What determines value?)
C. Leader continues:
   1. If you lost everything in a flood and your bank went bankrupt, what would you have left that was of any value?
   2. Do you see in others things which you consider valuable—in fact, so valuable that you, too, would like to possess them?
   3. Make a list of those things.
   4. Now, list all the possessions of value that you could give away to another person, and when you did so, would make both of you more valuable. (For example: love, trust, education)
   5. Develop a plan that you will follow to help you give those things away.
   6. Discuss with the group your plan of giving.
      a) Make suggestions to each other how those plans can best be carried out.
      b) Also try to discover for each other what things might occur in this process that will keep you from being successful. How can these things be overcome?
   7. As a group, decide the best plan of giving.

Summary and Conclusion:
Prepare a short drama to help you show the whole group how this giving could best be done.

My Ideal Friend

by David Freitag

Age: Junior High through High School

Setting: Large or small groups, Sunday school, evening activity, camp

Time: 45–60 minutes (depends upon size of group)

Goal: To help youth examine what qualities a friend should have and to determine whether these qualities measure up to God's standard

Leader Preparation: Paper and a pencil for each participant, Bibles, and a concordance for reference

Scripture: 1 Samuel 20

The Exercise:
1. Activity: Give each person a sheet of paper and a pencil. Have each make a composite drawing of the ideal friend. Let this drawing express the most important qualities of a friend. People may need to write words to clarify parts of their drawings.
2. Discussion: Have all explain their drawings. Have them tell why the qualities they included are important.
3. Activity: Read 1 Samuel 20 in an easy-to-understand version. Now, have each person make a drawing of Jonathan, listing and showing the qualities he displayed as a friend to David.
4. Discussion: Have each person share how their drawing of their friend compares with Jonathan. Ask: Would you make any changes in your drawing? Explain any changes you would make.

Summary and Conclusion:
    As a home assignment, make an honest drawing of yourself. How do you compare with Jonathan?

Exercise Twenty-Five

. . . .

People or Things?

by Gordon West

Age: Junior High through College

Setting: Three groups of 4–6 youths (This may be duplicated to provide more participation by repeating the assignments for more sets of small groups who will work simultaneously.)

Time: 45–60 minutes

Goal: To explore consequences of various situations by completing stories and, afterwards in group discussion, to express feelings about choosing between people and objects

Leader Preparation: Blank filmstrips and permanent markers for each group, stories to pass out to each group (pp. 83–85), slide projector, Bibles, and a concordance for reference

Scripture: Matthew 6:25–26; Luke 12:6–7

The Exercise:
   A. Divide the youth into small groups and give them the following instructions while you are passing out the materials.
      1. I will be giving each group some materials to equip you to be movie producers . . . well, almost! I want you to be as creative as possible.
      2. Each group will receive a different story to complete and share with the rest of the group at the end. We will also talk about the process we went through to decide how the story should end.
      3. Pick 1 person to draw the illustrations for the story on the filmstrip and another person to narrate the story when you show it.
      4. You have 15 minutes.

. . . .

B. When the stories and illustrations are prepared, have each group show and narrate its filmstrip.

C. After each group tells its story, open up discussion to the whole group to evaluate the options chosen in each situation. Have each group explain what process they went through to decide how to end their story. Have group members tell how they felt about the various options. Also see how other groups feel about the options.

Summary and Conclusion:

1. Which is more important—people or things?
2. What is the problem faced in each of these situations?
3. When are people more important than things?
4. When are things more important than people?
5. Which do you think God values more?
6. What makes you think so? What Scriptures could you base your opinion on?

Handouts for Groups

Group 1

Pick someone in your group to be the illustrator and another to record the story to be narrated later. As a group, decide how this situation should be played out. What are the various options the characters have? Use the film to tell the story!

Frame 1:   A thief is breaking into a house at night.

Frame 2:   The thief is carrying off a TV.

Frame 3:   The owner of the home wakes up and hears something.

Frame 4:   The owner reaches for a gun in the nightstand.

Frame 5:   The owner is taking aim at the thief.

Frame 6:   Complete the story. Does the homeowner shoot the thief? What are the important elements here? Do homeowners have the right to kill in order to protect their valuable property?

Use as many frames as you need to creatively complete this story, but be sure that your group agrees on how it should come out! Be ready to discuss the alternatives that you considered and the struggles your group had in deciding how to complete the story.

Group 2

Pick someone in your group to be the illustrator and another to record the story to be narrated later. As a group, decide how this situation should be played out. What are the various options the characters have? Use the film to tell the story!

Frame 1:   A mother and son are arguing fiercely.

Frame 2:   The son demands the right (which earlier had been tentatively agreed to) to purchase a used car for his own use.

Frame 3:   The son lists many reasons why he needs and deserves the car.

Frame 4:   The mother says she is scared and hurt.

Frame 5:   She gives reasons why she is afraid for the son to have a car.

Frame 6:   She is hurt that he would not obey her and she acts very upset.

Frame 7:   Complete the story. Do the mother's feelings matter? What about the son's rights and the earlier agreement? What are the options for each person? What is the right ending?

Use as many frames as you need to creatively complete this story, but be sure that your group agrees on how it should come out! Be ready to discuss the alternatives that you considered and the struggles your group had in deciding how to complete the story.

Group 3

Pick someone in your group to be the illustrator and another to record the story to be narrated later. As a group, decide how this situation should be played out. What are the various options the characters have? Use the film to tell the story!

Frame 1:   John and his friend George are discussing an upcoming school dance.

Frame 2:   John mentions two different girls he would like to ask. One is rich and pretty, and the other is average and fairly poor.

Frame 3:   John prefers the second girl as a friend, but George pressures him to ask the more "desirable" rich girl.

Frame 4:   John knows the richer girl would pay for the evening . . . and she *is* good looking. (He basically can't make up his mind.)

Frame 5:   The rich girl walks up to John and asks if he is going to the dance.

Frame 6:   Complete the story. What does John do? What should he do? What would you do? Does it matter that 1 is rich and the other poor?

Use as many frames as you need to creatively complete this story, but be sure that your group agrees on how it should come out! Be ready to discuss the alternatives that you considered and the struggles your group had in deciding how to complete the story.

Exercise Twenty-Six

Precious Stones

by Irving Jennings

Age: Youth through Adult

Setting: Group

Time: 40 minutes

Goal: To give students an opportunity to evaluate their desire for the fruits of the Spirit

Leader Preparation: Paper and pencils for each participant

Scripture: 1 Corinthians 12:31; Galatians 5:20

The Exercise:

Each of you take your paper and label it "rock mine." Now, draw ten rocks on that piece of paper. Make the rocks large enough so that you can put names on them. Now, label the rocks with the following: *love, faith, kindness, health, peace, knowledge, patience, family, wealth, friends. (Leader:* You may increase the number of rocks if you would like to include more traits or attributes.)

Now, we go out rock hunting. We drive out to the rock field and have to walk in about a mile. By the time we arrive at the field, you find that your side pack has come off. It's lost. So, you will have to carry all the rocks in your hands, and you are able to hold only five rocks. This means that you will have to look around and choose the five you want. Circle those five on your paper.

Now, we walk back to the car. On the way, you somehow lose one of your rocks. Because it is getting late and we have to get back before dark, you really can't go back to find the lost one. Now, I realize you usually don't get to choose what you are going to lose, but if you had a choice, which of your rocks would you choose to lose? Cross out the one that you lost and put an **L** by it.

About five miles from home, our car runs out of gas. Aren't we lucky there is a trading post and gas station just across the road? But, in order to have enough money to buy enough gas to get us home, you will have to sell two of your precious rocks to the trading post. Which two are you going to sell? Cross out those two, and put the letters **TP** beside them.

We are only a block away from home when you see a beggar on the side of the road. Even after all our troubles, the compassion in your heart makes you want to stop and give him one of your rocks. Which of your two remaining rocks are you going to give him? Go ahead and cross that one out too. Put a **B** by it.

Summary and Conclusion:

Divide up into groups of five and discuss why you chose the rocks that you did to start with and why you made the decisions you did from that point on. Introduce the Scripture listed, and encourage students to mention any others they feel are applicable. If there is enough time, go through it again and decide as a group what you would do. Then, come together briefly as a large group and share what your number-one choices were.

Leader: Note the different levels of moral reasoning. Also note the persistence or lack of it in the groups when they try to come to a group agreement.

The Prodigal's Return

by Holly Tales

Age: Junior High through College

Setting: Group

Time: 35–45 minutes

Goal: To make a Bible story apply to teens today; to teach responsibility and communication skills; to make youth aware of ways that their response to their parents can effect the outcome of a situation

Leader Preparation: Prepare four adult volunteers by going over the exercise in advance, having Bibles ready. Plan what you will do if this exercise stirs up a lot of feelings for some of the youth

Scripture: Luke 15:11–32

The Exercise:
- A. Read Luke 15:11–32.
- B. Ask for four volunteers to role-play the son (It works better to ask some of the more outgoing youth).
- C. The youth leader(s), or four more volunteers, will role-play different parenting styles and how they would react differently in the same situation.
  1. *Authoritarian:* Glad he's back, but now you lay down the law. He will have to mend his ways and follow your rules; perhaps ground him to make sure he knows that you are serious.
  2. *Neglectful:* No real reaction; hardly even mentions he was gone.
  3. *Permissive:* Be ecstatic he wasn't harmed; pamper him and let him know it's OK to be a jerk—the whole world revolves around him.
  4. *Authoritative:* Welcome him, but also let him know that his behavior was inappropriate and that he should have talked this out; be willing to discuss what caused him to leave.

D. Have a circle of chairs in each corner of the room, and let the youth divide up into four discussion groups based upon which style they think their parents would have adopted; have an adult in each group.

E. Let each group discuss how they feel when their parents react in that manner, how they usually react, and the general outcome.

F. Point out that the prodigal's father is both more strict and more lenient than the average parent. He does not rescue his son in the pigpen but lets him suffer until he truly repents. But the father also welcomes him back unconditionally, without laying a guilt trip on him for his former behaviors.

G. What would it feel like to have that sort of a parent? List the positives and the negatives.

Summary and Conclusion:

Let them discuss how they should react to their parents in accordance with Scripture. Take time to reread and examine the son's exact words when he got ready to return home. Role play it in a modern setting.

Homework: Use the method in the final role play to deal with parents the next time there is a conflict.

Exercise Twenty-Eight

. . . .

Who Decides Who I Am?

Age: Junior High through Adult (each age group will deal with these issues from a different developmental phase of values formation)

Setting: Group

Time: 2–7 one-hour sessions

Goal: To help participants think through their reasons for responding to authority as they do and to clarify what constitutes authority for them

Leader Preparation: Do you know people who are so concerned about what others think is right or wrong that they seem incapable of making a decision for themselves? Many people are so busy trying to be accepted by others that they have no values of their own. Most of our values are set when we are young. This exercise helps young people evaluate who is or has been setting their values: family, friends, school, church, or society itself. Adults can also benefit from periodically standing back and looking at their values and the things that clamor for importance.

By assessing their present values, group members can determine which values they hold in highest regard and evaluate all their other decisions and activities to see if they will help achieve the goals that matter most.

This will be a challenge because a person must examine values taught and practiced by friends, school, family, church, and society. Even more, a person has to look honestly at himself or herself—personal motives, weaknesses, and strengths. This honest work is necessary for anyone who is going to seriously determine his or her own values and create healthy autonomy.

Have an Insight Sheet (p. 93) for each participant. Also, determine in advance where you want to divide up the discussion issues so that you'll have a balanced number from session to session. One suggestion is to begin each session with question 1 and end each session with question 7. The issues raised in questions 2–6 could be stretched out over as many as six additional sessions or clustered into only two sessions.

. . . .

Scripture: Proverbs 4:23; Romans 12:1–2

The Exercise:
A. The Survey
   1. Explain that the survey looks at what we value and the things we let become authorities in our lives.
   2. Give each person a copy of the Insight Sheet (p. 93) and ask each to put a circle on the scale at the point that reflects where he or she is at this time and then to list two or three recent examples to back up that position.
   3. When participants have completed all the scales and listed their examples, have each put an X on the scale to show where he or she would like to be in two or three years.

B. Discussion Questions
   1. Have you ever sacrificed something you believed in to gain acceptance by a group (or a certain person)? Do you believe that your friends influence your values or help you create your values? If so, how do you feel about that? Have you ever seen this happen with anyone else? Give an example. What difference does it make what others think about what's important to me? Should it matter? Why or why not?
   2. What are some values you believe your parents have tried to give you—what's most important in your family? Have you accepted all or some of these values? Do your parents practice the values they say they want you to accept, or are there two standards being presented, one spoken and one lived out? Are there some values you already know you do not want to pass on to your own children? Are there some you'd be willing to die for?
   3. For Youth: What values are/are not being presented in your school? Have you ever heard the term *value-free education?* Do you think that this is possible? What are ways to get a value across without actually talking about it? How do the values from school compare or contrast with those from your home? How do school values and your friends' values differ? How are they the same?
   4. In what ways do you believe society's values have changed over the past ten years? Have changing social values affected your personal beliefs? (For example, the ecology movement, the women's movement, wars in various nations, sexual freedom) If so, in what way?
   5. Do the values expressed and developed by mass media and advertising influence what you consider valuable or important? Why or why not? What about the effect on your values of sports stars, musical groups, and TV shows? *Leader:* Prepare for this topic by cutting out ads from magazines that you know appeal to your group.

6. What kind of influence do the teachings of the church have on your choices and decisions about what you value in your day-to-day life and in your plans for the future? Do you feel the teachings of the church are relevant to modern society? In what way?

7. Do you believe Jesus Christ brought a unique set of values by which His followers are to live? What difference does it make if we do or don't live by them? Can you point out some similarities and differences between what Jesus says is important and what these other forces influence you to value? Is it even possible to live by the values that Jesus gave to us? What is God's opinion? Reflect and comment.

Summary and Conclusion:

Summarize the major areas of conflicting values that the group brought out in today's discussion. Read Proverbs 4:23 and Romans 12:1–2. Challenge them to invite God to help them understand what's really important and to make a commitment to live according to these values.

Insight Sheet

I.

1	2	3	4	5	6	7	8	9	10

I do things
because I decide
I want to do them.

I do things
because others
tell me what to do.

Examples: _____

II.

1	2	3	4	5	6	7	8	9	10

I do things I want to do
without considering what
others may think of me.

I always do things after
considering what others
will think of me.

Examples: _____

III.

1	2	3	4	5	6	7	8	9	10

I make my own
decisions about
what I am going to do.

I want to be told
what to do before
I do it.

Examples: _____

IV.

1	2	3	4	5	6	7	8	9	10

I only feel free
when I do the opposite
of what I'm told.

I only feel safe
when I do exactly
what I'm told.

Examples: _____

V.

1	2	3	4	5	6	7	8	9	10

To me, being different
means being unique and
especially valuable.

To me, being different
means being weird, a geek,
or an outcast.

Examples: _____

· ·

. . . .

Write Your Obituary

by Mervin Birky

Age: Youth through Adult (could be excellent for adults dealing with midlife issues)

Setting: Groups of 3–30 persons

Time: 40–50 minutes

Goal: To stand back and assign value to the components of one's life

Leader Preparation: Paper and pencils, discussion questions ready

Scripture: Ecclesiastes 12:13; Romans 12:3; 1 Peter 4:7–8

The Exercise:
   A. Imagine that you have just died. Your obituary will appear in tomorrow's newspaper. What will it say about you, your life, your death, your accomplishments and failures? You have 10 minutes to write a three-paragraph obituary for yourself.
   B. Get into groups of three. Trade papers and read the obituaries of the others in your group.
      1. For groups where people know one another:
         On the back of one other person's paper jot down your reaction to his or her obituary. Note changes you would make by deleting or making additions or by noting the things included that you would highlight.
      2. For groups where people do not know one another:
         Ask questions of one another that are aimed at
         a) Clarifying
         b) Expanding
         c) Gaining understanding of the facts included
      3. Allow 15 minutes for this part of the exercise.

. . . .

C. After all papers have been read, observations made, or questions asked, discuss the following (remaining in triads):
1. Changes and/or highlights made
2. What thoughts this exercise stirs up about your life
3. How this exercise makes you feel about your life
4. Things in the obituary of which you were most proud
5. Things in the obituary that you most regret
6. People whose influence has been powerful in making you the person you are

Summary and Conclusion:

Summarize on the bottom of your paper the 3 or 4 most significant things that make life meaningful for you.

Leader: Read the Scriptures above or other appropriate Scriptures.

Exercise Thirty

The Cost of Winning

by Steve Cummings

Age: Youth through Adult

Setting: Enough participants to divide into 6 groups of at least 3 persons each

Time: 45 minutes

Goal: To allow participants to experience a situation where there cannot be a win/win between the small team and the larger group (For the small team to "succeed" they must oppose the larger group); to evaluate the practical effect this has on Christian values

Leader Preparation: Understand the rules of the exercise so that you can explain them clearly without tipping off the participants to the parts they must learn by experience

Scripture: Ephesians 4:1–6

The Exercise:
1. Divide participants into 6 equal groups. "Now, I want you all to cooperate and work together in this exercise."
2. Each small group chooses a spokesperson.
3. Explain that this game is divided into 9 rounds, with an optional negotiation session available between rounds 3 and 4, and rounds 6 and 7. During the negotiation session, each group may, if they wish, send a representative to the negotiation table to confer with other groups' representatives.
4. During each round, each team must decide whether to vote for X or Y.
5. Don't give any other rules. Leave it up to the participants to figure out as they go along. Do not offer any reward or prize for winning.
6. This is how to score each round: If all 6 teams vote X, they each receive one point. If only 1 team votes Y and the other 5 vote X, the Y team gets

3 points, and the rest get 0. If 2 or more teams vote Y, everyone gets 0 points.

7. Eventually one team will realize that in order to earn the most points, they must be the only team to vote differently from the rest. In order to do this they must lie during negotiation sessions about how they plan to vote, deceiving the whole group.

Summary and Conclusion:
After tempers have settled, lead the group in a discussion:

1. First, make sure everyone is clear about how the game works and that it is a setup to pit groups against each other.
2. When did you start to realize what was going on—what was necessary in order to get the most points?
3. How did that make you feel?
4. How does this differ from a good game of basketball?
5. Did some find themselves being pulled into a competitive stance—wanting to win at all costs?
6. What forces in our daily lives influence us to win at all costs?
7. Read the Scripture from Ephesians (and any others you consider on target).
8. How does this Scripture compare with the competitive mind-set so common in our culture?
9. Is competition ever appropriate in the body of Christ? Why or why not? Under what circumstances?
10. What practical steps could increase cooperation in a situation you face this week?

Exercise Thirty-One

. . . .

Dirt Bike

by Conrad Smith

Age: Juniors through Junior High

Setting: Group

Time: 20–30 minutes

Goal: To focus on the value of honesty in all things, especially when cheating would be easy

Leader Preparation: A copy of the story to role-play, the discussion questions, and a Bible

Scripture: Exodus 20:15; Deuteronomy 5:19; Matthew 19:18; Romans 13:9–10

The Exercise:
   A. Have the children role-play this story:
          You and two other friends have been using your neighbor Charlie's minibike on the trails of a nearby park. You bike every chance you get and hope someday to be a dirt-bike racer. Charlie decides to sell the bike, and you and your friends decide to buy it. They already have their share of the money, but you have cleaned out all your savings and you are still $10.00 short.
          You go to your father's drugstore, and your father asks you to tend the store while he works in the storeroom. During this time, rich Old-Man Thompson comes in and buys a few items for a total of $9.83. Mr. Thompson complains that he's only going to get a few cents back in change. He can't see very well, and he thinks he's handing you a $10.00 bill. Actually, the bill in his hand is a $20.00 bill.
          Suddenly you realize that it would be easy to just let him think his $20.00 is a $10.00, and you could keep the extra $10.00, which is exactly what you need for that dirt bike! Your dad won't lose any money, and Mr. Thompson will never notice. He's rich, anyway.

. . . .

B. Discussion questions:
   1. Do you keep the money?
   2. What are the reasons you do or do not keep the money?
   3. What are the possible consequences of your decision?
   4. Would you feel guilty for enjoying the bike?
   5. Suppose the bike breaks. Do think that would be because you cheated Mr. Thompson?
   6. What if Mr. Thompson finds out he gave you a $20.00 bill?
   7. Is it right for him to be so rich and you not to be?
   8. What do you think about taking the money and paying it back in secret later on?
   9. Would you be proud of your decision?

Summary and Conclusion:

Have the students take turns looking up and reading aloud the Scriptures. End with Romans 13:9–10, and emphasize love being the reason behind all of the laws of God.

The Bionic Christian

by Warren Snyder

Age: Youth through Adult

Setting: Group

Time: 60 minutes

Goal: To elicit assumptions and present values about outward appearances and compare and contrast them with biblical standards

Leader Preparation: A Bible and paper and pencils (with erasers) for all participants; a board to summarize participants' responses will make this exercise much more effective

Scripture: 1 Samuel 16:7; Matthew 6:21

The Exercise:
  A. Tell participants, Draw a picture of a man or woman who, in your estimation, would look like the perfect Christian. As you are drawing, consider the following categories:
  1. The kinds of clothes he or she would wear.
  2. Facial features: hair style, glasses, hair color, etc.
  3. Physical stature: tall, short, heavyset, slender, etc.
  4. Intellect: logical, intelligent thinker; fairly intelligent; good with people but unable to think through the issues (the C student); not intelligent (D+ student) but with a tremendous servant's heart.
  5. Color of skin and nationality (you may have to revise your categories above).
  Be able to give reasons for the way you drew the figure.
  B. Next, draw a picture of a man who would look like Jesus Christ if He were to come to earth, during His First Coming, to your town this year. Use the categories in A to help construct your figure.
  C. Divide the large group into smaller groups of five and let participants

compare drawings. Let individuals choose one of the above categories and tell why they made the figure that way.

D. Reassemble the group to discuss the following issues:

Leader: Have your marker ready and start recording the various ideas the group expresses. On certain issues, take a vote and record the results (see below).

1. Should the "Bionic Christian" look the same as your figure of Jesus Christ? Why or why not?

2. Are certain kinds of hairstyles, clothes, or nationalities and skin colors more Christian than not? Compare your figure to a picture of a punk-rock guitarist that the masses admire. Do any of the media favorites look satanic? Does this really matter—i.e., is that a good enough reason for Christians to avoid them?

   Leader: Record the votes on this item after a show of hands.

3. Share any interesting ideas that came up in your smaller group.

4. Why does most of Scripture talk about the inner character qualities instead of outward appearance or clothing? What do the Scriptures say about clothing? (Jot any relevant Scriptures on the board.) Do we model the idea that Christians should dress a certain way when they go to church? Why or why not?

5. Just how should we dress modestly and discreetly so as not to draw attention to ourselves in this culture? (List the major ideas on the board.)

Summary and Conclusion:

1. *Leader:* Divide the board into four squares. Two will be for "time" and two will be for "money." Ask the group, "How much time do we as American believers spend on our outward appearance?" Have both males and females call out the average time per day they spend on shopping, grooming, working out, etc., and record the numbers in one of the time boxes. "It this right or wrong? Why?" Next, ask the group to call out the average amount of time they spend per day reading the Bible, praying, and serving God. Write this in the other time box. Compare the two time boxes. Based upon amount of time spent on each activity, which do we value more, the things of God or our outward appearance?

2. Using the other two boxes, make the same comparison with use of money. Compare the average amount of money the group spends on appearance in one month's time to the average amount they give to the kingdom of God. Based upon this data, which do we value more, inner beauty or outer?

Conclude with a reading of the Scriptures.

Exercises for Families

Exercice One

. . . .

Family Treasures

Source: Gospel Light Family Values Workshop

Age: Preschool through Elementary (child needs to be able to talk—probably most effective in a home with school-aged children)

Setting: Home; since there are 5 segments, a family could do 1 per night as part of a special values theme for a week

Time: 5–20 minutes per segment

Goal: To focus on values being established primarily in the home and to see the Bible as the foundation of all values

Leader Preparation: Drawing materials, copies of the exercise or a board to write it on, and poster paper or cloth for a flag

Scriptures: Deuteronomy 6:5–7; Matthew 6:19–21; Mark 12:28–31; Romans 12:2; Colossians 2:6–7

The Exercise:
1. Most Prized Possessions
    Think together of 2 or 3 items your family prizes. Grandma's china pitcher? your camping equipment? the piano? Draw pictures of most-prized possessions. Next, choose a quality about your family that you treasure—sense of humor, ability to express love toward one another, or the freedom your family allows for individuality. Write a line or two about a most-prized family quality.
2. Favorite Words
    What words do you most like to hear from others in your family? "I love you"? "That's OK"? Probably everyone in the family will want to make a "favorite words" card. Let young children tell their favorite words for a family member to write for them. Now have each family member tell the others why that is their favorite word.

. . . .

Building Biblical Values

3. Agree or Disagree?

    A   D   Values are what you say you believe.

    A   D   People reveal their values by their choices, their decisions, and their actions.

    A   D   Values are what you really care about—people, beliefs, possessions, ideas, activities, and how you use your time, energy, and money.

4. Biblical Values

From the Scriptures listed above, choose at least 3 statements that deal with Christian values you want to be important in your family. Now have each member explain those choices to the others in the family circle.

5. Family Sign

From the items that you've already discussed, get ideas to help you draw a family sign or flag. Be creative! Make the sign or flag a realistic symbol of who you are and what you like—a sign that would help someone understand what kind of people live at your house.

Summary and Conclusion:

As children discuss and participate in clarifying their family's unique values, they are more likely to find the strength to uphold those values in the face of outside opposition.

Exercise Two

· ·

50-Year Anniversary*

by John Cioncia

Age: Married Couples or Families

Setting: Could be used by individual couples, or as part of a couples' retreat or couples' fellowship group

Time: 30 minutes

Goal: To help couples compare and contrast their values and to compare values with behaviors

Leader Preparation: A copy of the Priority Questionnaire (pp. 107–8) available for each participant

Scripture: 2 Corinthians 5:10; Ephesians 5:15; James 4:14

The Exercise:

This exercise provides a way for couples to communicate about values. As we look back on life together after 10, 25, or even 50 years of marriage, what patterns will we see? Where have we invested our time and what priorities have we given to our spending?

Each participant gets a survey to fill out. The husband can mark his own responses with a circle. Then, he should try to guess what his wife's responses will be and mark those with a square. Likewise, the wife should mark her personal responses and try to predict her husband's choices with a different symbol. Either husband or wife may choose to add other issues at the bottom of this list. Spouses should not consult with each other while filling out the survey.

---

* For additional help, see Fritz Ridenour, *How to Decide What's Really Important*.

· ·

Summary and Conclusion:

After the survey is filled out, husband and wife share their responses with each other, an item at a time. Note especially any items you disagree on more than once. This is an area you probably will need to discuss in greater detail.

Finally, compare your written responses with current reality. For example, you may list a family budget as a priority yet not actually have one. As a couple, discuss any incongruities and commit yourselves to the Lord to make any needed changes. Look up the Bible verses and bring their influence to bear upon your discussion.

Priority Questionnaire

Directions: Circle the answer describing how you feel. Place a square around the letter that you predict reflects your spouse's feelings.

Code: U—Unnecessary   E—Extra
D—Desirable   H—Helpful
N—Necessary

1.	Life insurance	U	E	D	H	N
2.	Dinner out together once a week	U	E	D	H	N
3.	Credit cards	U	E	D	H	N
4.	Stereo set	U	E	D	H	N
5.	Opening home for Christmas hospitality	U	E	D	H	N
6.	Continued formal education after marriage	U	E	D	H	N
7.	Two cars	U	E	D	H	N
8.	Planning a family budget	U	E	D	H	N
9.	Pets	U	E	D	H	N
10.	Vacation once a year	U	E	D	H	N
11.	Long-term savings plan	U	E	D	H	N
12.	Being involved in the community	U	E	D	H	N
13.	Owning a camper	U	E	D	H	N
14.	Giving at least 10% to the church	U	E	D	H	N
15.	Family outings monthly	U	E	D	H	N
16.	Weekly Bible study for couples	U	E	D	H	N
17.	TV	U	E	D	H	N
18.	Wife works at her career	U	E	D	H	N
19.	Motorcycle	U	E	D	H	N
20.	Donations to charities	U	E	D	H	N
21.	Personal time with each child weekly	U	E	D	H	N
22.	Attending marriage seminars	U	E	D	H	N
23.	Three nights a week reserved for family time	U	E	D	H	N
24.	Complete set of china	U	E	D	H	N
25.	Dishwasher	U	E	D	H	N
26.	Neighbors over for dinner	U	E	D	H	N

· ·

27.	Attending church activities	U E D H N
28.	Owning a boat	U E D H N
29.	Supporting a missionary as a family	U E D H N
30.	Participating in or watching sports	U E D H N
31.	Going places with our child	U E D H N
32.	Consistent prayer together as a couple	U E D H N
33.	Serving at the church	U E D H N
34.	Regular Bible reading and prayer with the kids	U E D H N
35.	Music lessons	U E D H N

Other issues and choices

36.	_____	U E D H N
37.	_____	U E D H N
38.	_____	U E D H N
39.	_____	U E D H N
40.	_____	U E D H N

Exercise Three

• •

The Spirit of the Home

Age: Elementary or older

Setting: Home

Time: 30 minutes

Goal: To provide families with a method to examine attitudes and behaviors about the practical expression of Christian life in the home

Leader Preparation: A copy of the Family Spiritual Life Survey (pp. 109–10) for each family member, a large piece of paper, the family calendar; a Bible with concordance will be convenient

Scripture: Genesis 12:3b; John 4:53; Acts 16:31; Galatians 6:10; Ephesians 2:19; 1 Timothy 3:15

• •

Building Biblical Values

The Exercise:

1. Have each member of the family fill out the Family Spiritual Life survey below (pp. 109–10).
2. Note items rated satisfied or extremely satisfied. Note items rated dissatisfied or extremely dissatisfied. Is there any correlation between degrees of satisfaction among different family members?
3. Divide a piece of paper into three columns and place it where everyone can see it. In the first column list any strengths the entire family agrees upon. In the second list any weaknesses. In the third column list any items where family members differ dramatically in their ratings. How many items do you have in each column? Is the family able to tolerate differing evaluations of its spiritual effectiveness? What Scriptures might apply?

Summary and Conclusion:

Finally, is the family able to agree on an area of weakness they would like to pray about? The family can pray about this area daily for one month (for example, from March 23 to April 23). Write the finish date (April 23) on the calendar as a reminder, and at that time discuss as a family what you feel God is leading you to do about it.

Family Spiritual Life Survey

Circle the number that best expresses your personal feelings about your family. 1 = extremely satisfied, 2 = satisfied, 3 = no opinion, 4 = dissatisfied, and 5 = extremely dissatisfied.

1. I experience a high level of love and closeness in my family. 1 2 3 4 5
2. We share our feelings and needs in our family. 1 2 3 4 5
3. Conflicts between adults get worked out with mutual love and trust. 1 2 3 4 5
4. Each adult in the family is growing in Christ. 1 2 3 4 5
5. Adults take regular time to be with and to do things with children in the family. 1 2 3 4 5
6. Our family prays and shares spiritual things together. 1 2 3 4 5
7. We have Christian literature for adults in our home, and the adults read it. 1 2 3 4 5
8. We have Christian literature appropriate for the ages of the children in our home, and they read it. 1 2 3 4 5
9. The children are growing in their knowledge of Bible facts and their comprehension of the spiritual truths of the Bible. 1 2 3 4 5

10. It's easy to talk about God, His love, His truth, etc. in our home—for example, while watching a TV program.   1 2 3 4 5

11. Things I do at church have helped me this year to be a better member of my family (mom, dad, son, daughter, etc.).   1 2 3 4 5

12. We understand and apply in our home the things the Bible teaches about family living.   1 2 3 4 5

13. We have meaningful times of family devotions.   1 2 3 4 5

14. Discipline problems in our family get worked out so that poor behavior improves and children still feel loved and accepted.   1 2 3 4 5

15. Our church helps us understand and do what God wants in our family life together.   1 2 3 4 5

16. I feel sure the leaders of our church are alert to needs of families in general and care about our family in particular.   1 2 3 4 5

17. The parents have enough information about how to bring up children as growing Christians.   1 2 3 4 5

18. The husband is effective as head of our home.   1 2 3 4 5

19. Our church carefully sees that school-aged children are won to Christ and taught the Bible.   1 2 3 4 5

20. The family reserves at least one evening a week to be together—either at home or out together.   1 2 3 4 5

21. Our family knows enough about the Bible to train the children in spiritual things.   1 2 3 4 5

22. Our home reflects a loving, communicating atmosphere.   1 2 3 4 5

. . . .

Remember When

by J'Anne Stuckey

Age: Children

Setting: At home with family or during car trips

Time: 10–30 minutes (depends upon attention span of children)

Goal: For children to recognize that God watches over us and protects us from danger

Leader Preparation: 3 x 5 cards and a list of choices of Scriptures to memorize

Scripture: Deuteronomy 6:7

The Exercise:

Setup: This game is designed for a family to play together. Before playing, an adult prepares a number of 3 x 5 index cards with the following information: Each card lists one example of a time when God's watchful care was especially evident in the family's life. It could be when God was protecting one member of the family or when all of them were involved. Below that example, list several statements and questions such as: Tell us about the event. How did you feel when that happened? Word the questions to help the players focus on the feelings everyone had with that incident and on the way they experienced God's special love at that time.

An example:

The day lightning struck the house:

1. Tell us what happened.
2. How did you feel?
3. Did you talk to God about what was happening?
4. After that day, did you feel any differently about your family? About God?

. . . .

How to play: Keep the cards handy and pull them out when there is an opportune moment. Each family member takes turns drawing a card out of the pile and answers the questions. For the last question on the card, the player turns to the player on the left for an answer. The player on the left answers the last question and then draws a card and follows the same pattern. Play until all the cards are used up. The family adds new cards to the pile as new events occur. Parents can encourage children to share times of God's protection in their own lives and make a new card about it for the pile.

Summary and Conclusion:
Parents, choose a Bible verse about God's care and protection from the list you have prepared. Conclude each game by, as a group, memorizing one Scripture. Copy each newly memorized Scripture onto a 3 x 5 card and add it to the pile of game cards for review next time.

Exercise Five

. . . .

Sixteen Values

Adapted from the 1976 Commission of
Stewardship, National Council of Churches

Age: Junior High through Adult

Setting: Married couples, family groups, or individuals

Time: 20 minutes

Goal: To provoke participants to struggle with the rightness of their economic value system in the light of Scripture

. . . .

Leader Preparation: Lists of values (below) for each participant to rank

Scripture: Matthew 5 and 6

The Exercise:

People are not likely to change their values when their lives are calm and stable. But when there are profound changes in the social basis of life, the relative importance people place on values changes: old values start to seem less important and new ones emerge.

We are presently in such a time of change. The past several decades have seen new technologies, political and moral revolution, new voices clamoring for authority, the crumbling of traditional faiths, and the appearance of new creeds. Mass communication and frequent moving exposes us to a greater variety of cultures, faiths, and institutions, often with conflicting values.

All these factors have changed families, communities, and cultural patterns. Values come to us from family, friends, schools, religions, businesses, and television. The family and other traditional sources of values have, in many instances, lost their ability to shape values. The result is confusion and conflict about values on the part of both individuals and the family unit.

Furthermore, what we say we believe and the beliefs we act upon frequently do not match.

The following exercise will be a useful tool to help individuals become more aware of what their gut-level values are and then, as results are shared, to communicate those values to others. For family groups or married or engaged couples, this can provide a kick-off for honest discussion about differing priorities. Do the work alone. Then talk over the results with another person, your family, or with a group.

Two scientists, Milton Rokeach and Seymour Parker, have worked out the following list of sixteen values:*

- A comfortable life
- An exciting life
- A sense of accomplishment
- A world at peace
- Equality
- Family security
- Freedom
- Happiness

- Inner harmony
- Mature love
- National security
- Pleasure
- Self-respect
- Social recognition
- True friendship
- Wisdom

---

* Milton Rokeach and Seymour Parker, "Values As Social Indicators of Poverty and Race in America," *The Annals of the American Academy of Political and Social Science* 388 (March 1970): 97–111.

From this list, select the five values you prize most highly. Rank order these five values, 1–5. Put a dollar sign ($) by those you selected that require money or influence the use of money. Reflect on your reasons and feelings in selecting and ranking as you did.

Summary and Conclusion:
Talk over your results with at least one other person. Brainstorm any Scriptures that relate to any of the items you chose. Think about whether any of your values are negotiable or open to change. How will you and your family deal with differing priorities? Could God get you to change your mind?

Exercise Six

• •

Your Dollars Are Worth More Than You Think

Adapted from a technique by Dorothy Z. Price*

Age: High School through Adult

Setting: Individuals, couples, or families with adolescents

Time: About 45 minutes, unless the group decides to do the Bible study too; a better plan might be to schedule a second session for an in-depth Bible study on this topic.

Goal: To stimulate participants to better understand the financial choices they make.

Leader Preparation: A copy of the Economic Value Statements survey (pp. 116–18) and pencils for all

---

* This technique for analyzing the economic value system was adapted from a research project at Washington State University. For further information refer to Dorothy Z. Price, "A Technique for Analyzing the Economic Value System," *Journal of Marriage and the Family* (August 1968): 467–72.

• •

Scripture: 1 Timothy 6:6–11

The Exercise:
  There are seventy-five statements requiring a response. You may find it difficult to judge some statements on the scale. Use your first impression, your immediate feeling, to decide what to mark. Do not look back and forth through the items. Judge each statement—do not omit any item.

Summary and Conclusion:
  All of the statements that you circled are beliefs related to a value. The letter preceding each statement is your clue to the following values:
  (A) Status (concerned with spending money for prestige)
  (B) Security (values money for itself as a symbol of security)
  (C) Self-actualization (sees money in relationship to how it helps people fulfill themselves)
  (D) Self-indulgence (spending money is gratifying and feels good)
  (E) Economic faith (unconcern regarding money; no reason to worry about money)

To total up your score:
Count the number of (A) statements for which you circled 1 and enter below. Count the number of (A) statements you circled 2 and enter below, etc.

		1	2	3	4	5
1.	Number of (A) statements circled:	____	____	____	____	____
2.	Number of (B) statements circled:	____	____	____	____	____
3.	Number of (C) statements circled:	____	____	____	____	____
4.	Number of (D) statements circled:	____	____	____	____	____
5.	Number of (E) statements circled:	____	____	____	____	____

  As you analyze the scores above, which values are most likely to influence your financial decisions? How does this line up with what the Bible says about material resources?
  Leader: If this is a group, have the participants use Bibles (and concordances if necessary to locate passages) to look up Scriptures to defend (or refute) each of the 5 values (A–E above). List the results on the board for people to ponder.

Economic Value Statements

Please give your answers according to your own judgments, your own value system, your own philosophy. Use the following numbering system:

1	Most like me	4	Slightly unlike me
2	Slightly like me	5	Least like me
3	Neutral or Not applicable		

_____(A) Clothes should look expensive.

_____(A) A fancy car and a good-looking house spell success.

_____(B) Thrifty people manage best.

_____(D) It would be easy to spend $5000 in just a couple of days.

_____(C) The purpose of money is to serve the family—not to be served by the family.

_____(C) It's all a matter of deciding what things are most important and then planning outgo to fit income.

_____(D) A list of "things to buy someday" is usually endless.

_____(E) Live with confidence in the future and the help of the installment plan.

_____(E) Just wait and money problems either go away or take care of themselves.

_____(A) A big income means that a person has really arrived.

_____(A) A person has to look successful.

_____(B) Having no cash savings is frightening.

_____(B) Look around until you find the best price.

_____(B) Don't buy until you have to have something; then try to be sure.

_____(C) It's hard to see why people would let themselves become slaves to money.

_____(E) No system or plan—if you're spending too much, just stop.

_____(D) If you want something, you should have it right now.

_____(C) Money doesn't buy happiness.

_____(B) There should always be a good balance in the checkbook for emergencies.

_____(D) A person is entitled to some of the "nice things" from life.

_____(E) If there's a really serious financial problem, someone will always help.

_____(A) Children should live in a neighborhood that will bring them into contact with important people.

_____(A) Money and prestige—they go hand in hand.

_____(B) When the price of something you need is "2 for 1," it's always best to get 2.

_____(D) It's terrible to have to wait for something you really want.

_____(C) There are a lot of things more important than money.

_____(B) Every penny should be carefully watched.

_____(D) Money is to spend.

. . . .

Building Biblical Values

_____(A) You must spend a little more than you can afford to get ahead in life.

_____(E) If you need money, it will come from somewhere.

_____(D) There will always be more things to do than there is money to do with.

_____(C) Enough money to live comfortably, but not necessarily luxuriously—that's enough for happiness.

_____(B) A certain amount of money should be allotted for each item each month.

_____(A) Nothing is too good for one's children.

_____(C) It seems silly to try to keep up with the Joneses.

_____(E) Worrying about money never helps.

_____(B) Spend only for necessities.

_____(A) None of that cheap stuff is worth much.

_____(C) We spend our money on what we care most about.

_____(B) Don't buy anything unless there's enough money to pay for it.

_____(E) Live from paycheck to paycheck and don't fret about it.

_____(D) No matter how much you have, you want more.

_____(A) A good address is really necessary.

_____(C) It's easy to have fun with simple things that are not necessarily connected with spending money.

_____(D) Happiness is buying something brand new.

_____(A) I'd like to have nothing but the best.

_____(E) A person can get along without saving.

_____(D) The more money you make, the less you have left.

_____(C) Children should learn not to put a dollar value on everything.

_____(D) What did people ever do before credit?

_____(A) Buying at the best stores is important.

_____(C) Education, the warmth of a family life, trips together, shared pleasures—these are the real products of a family.

_____(C) It's nice to make gifts even when you can afford to buy them.

_____(E) Why worry about money?

_____(A) If you have to scrimp and save, other people shouldn't know.

_____(D) Does anyone ever really have enough money or things?

_____(C) A lot of money would be nice but not really essential.

_____(A) Children should go to the top schools. Cost is secondary.

_____(E) Why even try to make any plans about money?

_____(D) It would be wonderful to be a millionaire—all that money just to spend.

_____(D) Walking through stores can be depressing. There's so much you see that you'd like to have.

_____(C) If the choice is between a job with long hours and high income and one with a somewhat lower income and more time for oneself, the second one will be far better.

_____(A) At a restaurant it's nice to be the one who picks up the check for the whole group.

_____(C) It doesn't make sense to want the best, the nicest, the shiniest just because it is the best, the nicest, and the shiniest.

· ·

Exercises for Families   117

____(E) There's no need to worry even if there isn't a cent in the bank.

____(D) What's more fun than just spending money.

____(B) It's important to record every penny spent, even down to postage stamps and chewing gum.

____(E) You can get by without insurance or hospitalization—just count on your guardian angel.

____(B) Paying in cash is the best way.

____(E) Keeping track of every penny and nickel can drive a person crazy.

____(B) A person can't have too much insurance.

____(E) A budget is only for someone who thinks money is everything.

____(B) Every debt should be cleared up as one goes along.

____(E) There's no need to budget. Either you have it or you don't.

Exercise Seven

· ·

Car Money or Kind Mercy?

by James McKean

Age: Couples or Families

Setting: Family group at home or an all-ages Sunday school class

Time: 30–45 minutes

Goal: To stimulate families to think through their values about money and to apply scriptural principles to modern-day situations

Leader Preparation: A copy of the exercise, questions to stimulate discussion, Bible and concordance for reference

· ·

Scripture: Matthew 6:33; 1 Corinthians 12:24b–26; Galatians 6:7–10; Philippians 2:13, 4:19; 1 John 3:17

The Exercise:
  A. Role-play the following story:

> The Jones family has decided they need a new car. They started saving money each month to be able to buy one. By now, they almost have enough money saved up.
>
> Then, they hear about another family from their church—the Smith family. The Smiths are in a lot of financial trouble. The father is out of work, and the mother is very sick and needs an operation at the hospital.
>
> Have the family act out the scene for both the Joneses and the Smiths.

  B. Now, read each of the Scriptures above, as well as any others you can apply to this situation. Make sure everyone understands the verses, substituting modern words or explaining the meanings of words when necessary.
  C. Discuss the following issues:
  1. List reasons to buy a new car.
  2. List reasons to help another family.
  3. List reasons not to buy a car.
  4. List reasons not to help the other family.
  5. Is it a good thing to help other Christians who are in distress?
  6. Would it be better to make a loan or to give an anonymous gift? Why?
  7. What will be the long-term consequences if the Jones family does give the Smith family the car money? If they don't?
  8. If they give away the money, how will they manage without a new car? How badly do they need it? Could they get a good used car instead?
  9. How will we decide, finally, what to do? What if we all cannot agree?

Summary and Conclusion:
  1. Is it all up to us or will God help us?
  2. What does the Bible say God does with people who give their money away to help other people?
  3. Look up 2 Corinthians 8 and 9 and read aloud portions that apply.

Conclude with prayer for the Holy Spirit to teach us His will (Philippians 2:13).

Exercises for Children

Exercise One

. . . .

Father God

by Ed Tafilowski

Age: Grades 4–9 (but try to have children in the group be close to the same age)

Setting: Small group Bible study or Sunday school

Time: 30–45 minutes

Goal: To help children realize and appreciate God's right to exercise authority in their lives, laying a foundation for greater obedience

Leader Preparation: From a concordance, a list of key Scriptures that refer to God as being like a father or being our Father (Some of these references are listed for you below, but there are also many more); a Bible for each student and a chalk board or large sheet of paper to write on; also, copies of the questions for each student or have the questions up on the board where they can be referred to easily

Scripture: Psalm 103, 19:11; Proverbs 11:18; Matthew 5:43–6:18; Galatians 6:7–8; Hebrews 11:6

The Exercise:
   A. First introduce the idea of a connection between the ideas of father and of God. See if the students can remember any Scriptures that connect these two ideas.
   B. Next, quickly review the prepared questions below:
      1. Why do you think God is often called "Father" in the Bible?
      2. When you think of a good father, how do you picture him?
      3. Who can you think of from the Bible that had a good relationship with the heavenly Father?
      4. What was the reason for this good relationship?
      5. What happens in Scripture when someone disobeys God?

. . . .

6. Why would God, a good Father, want you to obey His rules?
7. Is it more important to do what God says is right than to do what your friends want? Why?
8. If you love and obey your heavenly Father, what will He do with you?
9. What sorts of things that children do does God reward? What sorts of things might He punish?
10. Is there anyone above God in authority who is more important to obey? Why or why not?

C. Now bring out your list of Scriptures and assign one or more to each child to look up. Let the children take turns reading the passages, and as they do, let the others pick out parts that would answer the questions on the list. (For example, a good father takes pity on his children, Psalm 103.) If the class is a typical Sunday school class with some Bible teaching in the past, some of the answers will be common knowledge. But it is also important to direct the children to the Scriptures and let them dig out some specific nuggets of truth for themselves. As the children dig out these fatherly attributes, write them up on the board for everyone to see.

Summary and Conclusion:

Children conclude by using the facts listed on the board to offer sentence prayers of thanksgiving to God for His fatherly attributes.

Exercise Two

Fool's Gold

by Bob Cook

Age: Grades 3–7

Setting: Ideally, have as many children in the group as the age of the children (e.g., 8 eight-year-olds, 10 ten-year-olds)

Time: About 45 minutes

Goal: To help children think through the source of the values they put on things

Leader Preparation: Print up play money. These bills will not have any numbers on them but rather symbols. There should be eight different designs of bills with eight different symbols in the middle: key, lightbulb, cup, heart, flower, snake, flag, and car. Make enough bills so that you have about fifteen times as many bills as children playing the game. Have a Bible in an easy-to-understand translation, with the necessary passages marked and ready.

Scripture: Proverbs 11:24; Matthew 19:23; Mark 10:25; Luke 12:16; 18:23

The Exercise:
1. To begin the game, throw all the money up in the air and let the children pick it up! It is not really important that the money be distributed evenly.
2. Next, the children will have one minute to decide which bills are of value and which are not. At this time in the game the value can be completely arbitrary—whatever the children decide.
3. Next, each child tries to accumulate as much "value" as possible within the next 10–15 minutes by trading or giving away bills. Encourage them to do their best to convince each other why a trade would be beneficial. They are free to circulate around the room, gaining value any way they can except by violence. However, they may not throw away any "bad" bills.

4. They are also free to trade with you, the leader, called the "bank." You will trade them one of anything for five of anything else. For example, if they want a flag, they must give you five of anything else before you will give them a flag.
5. At the end of 15 minutes (or sooner if action is lagging), call a stop. All the trading ends. Then, you announce the "true" or "correct" value for each bill, and let the kids add up their scores. For example, you may decide to set a flag at 3 points, a lightbulb at 5, etc. (As the leader, these values are entirely up to you.)
6. The values you announce as leader are final, no matter what each person thought the values would or should be. The highest score wins the game.

Summary and Conclusion:
1. Ask several of the children why they placed the values they did on certain bill patterns.
2. Ask everyone: Were you surprised at how it ended up? Do you think the final standard was fair? Why or why not?
3. Ask the winners: What kind of strategy did you use to come out ahead?
4. Ask everyone: Did you play by the values you really believed to be right or by the values you thought should be or probably would be right? Was any of it worth all the fuss over it? Was anyone disappointed with this game?
5. Now, tell the group they are not the only people to be surprised by having the things they value fool them. Read the parable of the rich fool (Luke 12:16–21) and the story of the rich young ruler (Luke 18:18–25) to the group.

Conclude by reading Matthew 6:19–21 to see what Jesus says about value choices that won't be a disappointment.

Exercise Three

Lost Wallet

by Alan Knott

Age: 7–10 years old

Setting: Group

Time: 30 minutes

Goal: To give an opportunity to children to examine and clarify the reasons they obey; for example, is it because of punishment and reward or because it's what everyone expects, or is it because I am convinced myself that it is the right thing to do? (While persons in this stage of moral reasoning will have limited ability to make autonomous decisions, it can be helpful for them to begin to clarify their reasons for moral behavior.)

Leader Preparation: Attempt to guide the thinking, affirm the responders, and create an atmosphere of acceptance

Scripture: Deuteronomy 22:1–4 in a translation that's easy to understand

The Exercise:
This exercise can be done either as a skit or simply told as a story. Try to have the students imagine they are the one in the story who found the wallet.

One day, you find a wallet on the sidewalk. There is $200 in the wallet. It's exciting to see so much money. Visions of what $200 could buy begin to dance in your head. (Here, get the children to suggest items.) It could buy a new bike or a BB gun or maybe a doll house. As you keep looking through the wallet, you come to the driver's license, and the picture of the person who owns the wallet seems to stare at you. You feel an inner tension begin between a desire to have what $200 could buy and the idea to locate the wallet's owner and return the wallet and the money.

Summary and Conclusion:
Use the following questions to stimulate group discussion after the story:
1. What is the right thing to do in this situation?
2. What is the wrong thing to do?
3. What are the feelings deep inside concerning what you really want to do?
4. What are your reasons for doing the right thing?
5. What are your reasons for doing the wrong thing?
6. If there were no way you could be punished for taking the money (but it was still wrong), would you take the money?

Read and discuss Deuteronomy 22:1–4. What does God say about lost items?

Exercise Four

. . . .

Honesty Quiz

by Susie Hayes

Age: 10–11 years old

Setting: Group

Time: 15–30 minutes

Goal: To make students aware of the value of honesty and how it applies to their daily lives

Leader Preparation: Be aware of where to find passages on honesty in the Bible; a Bible and a good concordance ready; a copy of the Honesty Quiz (p. 129) for each student

. . . .

Scripture: Proverbs 14:5; Acts 5:3; Colossians 3:9

The Exercise:
Have students complete the Honesty Quiz and then discuss their answers.

Summary and Conclusion:
1. Was it easier to tell the truth about Lucy than about Bobby? Why? Should that affect our decision?
2. Would you have a responsibility to offer the information you had learned that would affect the accusation against Jeff? What about all the times he didn't get caught?
3. Shouldn't we protect the ones we care about, even if it means lying or shading the truth? Why?
4. What does *honesty* mean? Do we always have to be completely honest? Why?
5. What is the difference between honesty and bluntness (or tact); between honesty and being discreet; between honesty and a white lie?
6. What does the Bible say about honesty? Work with students to use the concordance and look up verses under *honesty, liars, truth,* etc. List the most helpful verses on the board and pick one to memorize.

Honesty Quiz

Check the answer that comes closest to the way you feel you would react. Remember, be honest!

1. Lucy, the girl who sits next to you in class, is always telling lies about you to her friends during recess. One day you see Lucy cheating on the geography test. What would you do?

      _____ Ignore it because it's none of your business.

      _____ Tell your best friends after class.

      _____ Report her to the teacher.

2. Time after time, Jeff, the school bully, gets by with destroying school property. One day he is called to the principal's office because he is suspected of breaking a window. In the lunchroom you overhear some kids talking about who really did break the window. What would you do?

      _____ Ignore it.

      _____ Tell your friends you know who really broke the window.

      _____ Go directly to the principal.

3. Your best friend is going to flunk history if he doesn't pass the exam. What would you do?

      _____ Plan ahead of time to let him copy your paper during the test.

      _____ Study with him the week before (even though it means missing baseball practice and not playing in the upcoming game).

      _____ Pray for him, and leave it up to God.

4. Your friends want you to go with them to a movie of which your parents disapprove. You really want to go with your friends. What would you do?

      _____ Sneak out and go with your friends.

      _____ Tell your parents you are going to a different movie (of which they approve) and then go ahead with your friends.

      _____ Tell your friends you can't go (although they probably won't ask you to go with them again).

5. You are baby-sitting for the lady next door. She tells you her son, Bobby, must be in bed by 8:30 P.M. or he will not be able to go to the zoo tomorrow. Bobby is really a cute little kid. After you tuck Bobby in bed at 8:30, he sneaks out of bed because he wants you to rock him to sleep with his teddy bear. When his mother comes home, she asks if Bobby was in bed by 8:30. You know if you tell her he got up after 8:30, Bobby will not be able to go to the zoo. What would you do?

      _____ Tell her Bobby went to bed at 8:30 and never got up again.

      _____ Tell her Bobby did go to bed without telling her that he got up again.

      _____ Tell her Bobby went to bed on time, but that he did get up again.

Exercise Five

. . . .

Facing Crisis—
A Drama

by Sue Adolph

Age: Elementary

Setting: A group of boys and girls, or a fun project for a gathering of extended family during holiday get-togethers or summer vacations

Time: About 30 minutes

Goal: To help children value the nearness of God and His personal care for us, even in crisis situations

Leader Preparation: The story, discussion questions, and Scriptures ready to read; also fun to have some nautical props available such as a captain's hat, sailor hats, a rubber boat, binoculars, sunglasses, a shark's fin, waves, etc.

Scripture: Psalm 4:3; 145:18; Luke 18:1; Hebrews 4:15–16

The Exercise:

This is a drama based upon a family's experience. To begin, assign each part of the drama to a different person in your group and hand out the appropriate props. In a small group each child can have a part. In a larger group some children will have to be "the audience."

The narrator is the "mother." As she goes through the story, when each character is named, he or she should stand up and silently act his or her part out without interrupting the flow of the story.

The characters:

>   Sam, age 8, and Joe, age 10, brothers
>   Beth, age 6 and Amy, age 7 $\frac{1}{2}$, cousins of Sam and Joe
>   Daddy; Mother, narrator

. . . .

Uncle Jim and Aunt Margie
The captain
The shark
The man with the binoculars
God

The story-drama (Mother is the narrator):
Remember last summer when we were all on Daddy's boss's yacht getting ready to sail off to Bermuda for a vacation? We couldn't wait to leave. Remember how we could hardly sleep the night before because we were so excited? We were excited, but we were scared, too, because we'd never been on such a long boat trip before.

On the third day of the trip, Aunt Margie was alone downstairs, and we were all upstairs on the deck reading, playing, or fishing. Then we heard her screaming, so we all rushed downstairs. There we found her standing in six inches of water. The boat was flooding!

We all rushed to the deck to tell the captain. He radioed for help, but there was no answer! Meanwhile, the water kept coming into the boat, higher and higher! Our worst fears were coming true!

Wildly, we raced around to find our life preservers and put them on, while Daddy and Uncle Jim inflated three life rafts. By the time the rafts were inflated, the yacht was almost half-filled with water. We didn't have a chance to take anything into the rafts with us. Everyone was shouting. It was confusing and scary.

For the first time, we all began to realize we might die. Remember how we felt as we saw the raft with Aunt Margie, Uncle Jim, and you girls disappear behind a wave? Then, fifteen minutes after that, we lost view of the raft the crew were on.

We were alone and helpless with no food, no paddles, no water. Surely we were going to die. All we could do was pray. Nothing we could do would save us.

After two days of floating in the intense sun, our strength was fading away. But Daddy was still so sure God would take care of us—that He had heard our prayers and was going to save us.

Immediately after Daddy had prayed for us, while we were still holding hands, there was a big bump from underneath the life raft. It was so powerful it bounced Sam to the other side where Daddy was sitting. Remember how scared you were, and how you started to cry? Suddenly we saw the dorsal fin of a shark and realized the shark wanted us for dinner. Terrified, we held perfectly still and prayed and prayed. Miraculously, the shark swam away.

We were frantic, but we were also exhausted, and you kids had fallen asleep by this time. Daddy and I kept praying. Then, to our amazement, a ship came into view and kept getting closer! It was about half a mile away, when suddenly, it seemed to turn toward us! Later, we found out that the man who had binoculars had been looking on the other side of the ship. He got an urge to walk to our side of the cabin and look out. That was when he spotted us!

Within half an hour we were safely aboard the ship and in their hospital quarters. That ship was able to find the other two life rafts within three hours, before darkness came. What an answer to prayer! We had never been so close to death nor had we seen God work in such a miraculous way.

Summary and Conclusion:

It turned out that each all the children thought they were being punished because they had been disobedient to their parents. Sam had been told he could not bring his portable video game on the trip, but he had hidden it in his dufflebag anyway. Joe had been told to leave the lawnmower full of gas for the neighbor to mow the lawn while they were gone and to lock up all the bikes, but he hadn't bothered to do it. Beth had been playing with her mother's sunglasses and broken them. She didn't tell her mother when they were still on land and her mother could have bought another pair before they left. Amy had taken some money from Beth's piggybank; she was pretty sure Beth wouldn't notice because she was younger and couldn't count very well. They believed God would not answer their prayers because they had been too bad to get an answer! As a result, each child expected to die and was amazed when everyone was finally rescued.

1. Would it be hard for you to believe God would answer your prayers? Why?
2. What else could you have done in the situation besides pray?
3. What would have happened if you had done some of those things?
4. What things have you prayed for in your life?
5. Is praying to God something we should do every day?
6. What are some things we can pray about today? Let's pray about them now.

Sharing Cookies

by Mark Rich

Age: 6–10 years old

Setting: Sunday school, Christian day school, VBS, or camp

Time: 30 minutes

Goal: To show the children the value in sharing

Leader Preparation: For each child, 2 large cookies, 1 cup of icing, 1 plastic knife to spread the icing, and a piece of waxed paper upon which to work; also, on a tray in the center of the table, an assortment of sprinkles and cookie decorations such as red-hots, etc. (Prudent teachers will also have moist paper towels ready for spills)

Scripture: Proverbs 21:26; Ephesians 6:1

The Exercise:
1. Arrange students comfortably around tables to work on their cookies.
2. Give each student 2 large, plain cookies (oatmeal or sugar cookies, for example), a cup of icing, and a plastic knife.
3. Explain that the students may decorate each of the cookies with the supplies available but may not eat them. Instead, when the decorating is done, students should await further instructions.
4. Students will have opportunities to make their cookies more interesting by sharing icings and by sharing from the tray of decorations in the middle of each table.
5. After the cookies are decorated, ask the students to pick out just 1 of their 2 cookies to share, and have them go to another classroom (prearranged) to share this cookie.
6. Students now return to their own room to enjoy their remaining cookie.

Summary and Conclusion:
1. What was it like, trying to decorate your cookie? Did you have a hard time getting the decorations you wanted to use?
2. How did sharing your cookies with the other children make you feel?
3. Did you have one cookie you liked better than the other? If so, which one did you choose to share? Why?
4. Why do people usually feel good after they share?
5. What are some other ways you can share with others?
6. Conclude by reading the Scriptures out of *The Living Bible* or another paraphrase that will make the meaning easy for children to understand.

Exercise Seven

· ·

Not Judging by What We See

by Betty Jamison

Age: Preschool through Grade 3

Setting: Group (will work best with 2 teachers)

Time: 10–15 minutes: 5 minutes to examine the items and 5–10 minutes for discussion, depending upon age of children

Goal: For children to discover that judging from outward appearance can be deceptive; thus, they will begin to look beyond the surface of things, more like God does

· ·

Leader Preparation: Scriptures ready to read and the following items:

- Pretty perfume bottle filled with strong-smelling vinegar
- One Spanish comic book and one in English, with the covers switched
- Box in which tea bags come, filled with cookies instead
- Cookie box (empty)
- An attractive ball that is too flat to use
- Salt shaker with sugar in it
- Other similar items the teaching team may dream up

Scripture: 1 Samuel 16:7; Luke 6:37–38

The Exercise:
1. Display the items and allow 2 or 3 children at a time to examine them. Ask them to think about which one looks like something they would want, and let them examine it more closely; then let them check out the other items.
2. While another group of children takes its turn at examining the display, teacher takes the first group off to talk about what they saw. Why did they choose the item they did? What had they expected? When they looked at the item more closely, what did they discover?
3. Have them decide what they learned from this. Guide them to the central idea that the package does not always tell the contents.

Summary and Conclusion:
With all the children together have a discussion.*
1. Ask the children to share examples from their own experience when they misjudged someone or something by looking only on the external appearance.
2. Transition to judging people by giving an example where judging a person led to a misleading result (for example, thinking someone was stuck-up and unfriendly who was really shy, and who turned out to be a great friend once you stopped ignoring him or her; a baby brother doesn't like ice cream at first because it's cold, and he misses out on a treat). Show how this type of judging made you miss out on something enjoyable.
3. Ask children for examples of when judging by appearance led to the wrong conclusion, or when they were misjudged by others.
4. Read 1 Samuel 16:7 and briefly tell about David's being overlooked

---

*Note: If teachers feel it is appropriate for this group, use the lesson as reinforcement for safety training of children. Under discussion item 2, teacher can give as an example the nice-looking man who offers candy and a ride in his car but is not nice to children.

because he was considered too young, yet God had already chosen David to be the future king.

5. Discuss the benefits that come to us from not judging on outward appearance and the harm that comes when we do.

Read Luke 6:27–28 and conclude with prayer that God would help us to be more like Him, not judging others incorrectly, but taking the time to pray and look on the heart.

Exercise Eight

· ·

God Says

by Becky McKenna

Age: Preschool

Setting: Group

Time: About 10 minutes—explanation: 2 minutes, playing time: 4–5 minutes, and discussion: 3–5 minutes (This schedule conforms to the short attention span of this age level. The class can repeat the game later on, however.)

Goal: To help young children to value obeying God's Word and to practice an obedient response (Because younger children do not respond very well to the challenge of cognitive disequilibrium, this will keep them in the preconventional stage but will teach them to obey authority.)

Leader Preparation: A list of simple, concrete commands from Scripture and appropriate actions children can use to respond to each one

Scripture: James 1:22

· ·
Building Biblical Values

The Exercise:

Teacher holds up the Bible and says, "This is God's Word. In the Bible, God tells us how to live good lives. God is very happy when we do what He says. We're going to play a game. God tells us to love our friends, so when I say, 'Love your friend,' you give the person a hug, like this." (Teacher demonstrates and has the class try it.) "God also wants us to help our friends, so when I say, 'Help your friend,' you pick up a toy and put it away for your friend.

"God also wants us to obey our moms and dads, so when I say, 'Obey your mom or dad,' you say, 'Yes, Mom' or 'Yes, Dad.'" With each command, the teacher demonstrates it and has the children do it. After explaining the game, it will be helpful to repeat the four commands and demonstrate them again.

Now, the teacher alternates the four commands and the children respond with the actions they learned.

Summary and Conclusion:

Conclude by asking the children these questions:

1. How else can you love or help your friend?
2. How do you feel if you do not obey your parents?
3. How can you help your parents?

Variations:

1. Add more commands for older children, or vary the commands to fit a particular lesson or topic. Think of more commands and responses to fit them.
2. With older children introduce a challenge. Omit the words "God says" and add a silly, inappropriate command they should not respond to (similar to Simon Says). This variation may confuse young children, however, so stick to the positive aspect with them.

Obedience's Surprise

by Steve Cummings

Age: Grades 4–8

Setting: Class; a good follow-up for a lesson on obedience, either how Jesus came to obey His Father God and do His will (for Junior High) or, for junior-aged children, the story of the boy Samuel being called to obey God because Eli's sons had been disobedient

Time: 15–30 minutes

Goal: To show the value that obedience is beneficial regardless of the external circumstances

Leader Preparation: Have the drama ready

Scripture: Psalm 40:8; Proverbs 25:12; Isaiah 1:19; Hebrews 5:8; 11:6; 1 Peter 1:14

The Exercise:
Designate children to play the roles in the drama while you read it to the class.
The Drama:
Johnny wants to go to a skateboard show at the park, but his skateboard is broken. He comes home from school and sees a note on the refrigerator from his mother. She has wanted him to clean his room for several days now. He assumes that is what the note is about, so he doesn't read it.
(*Ask the class:* What would you do? Read the note or ignore it?)
Later, after the park is closed, Johnny's mother comes home and asks him if he read the note. He says "No." She is surprised, but she sends him to get the note and read it. Sure enough, the note asks him to clean his room, especially under the bed.

Now, with his mother there, Johnny obeys, so he goes off to clean his room. When he cleans under his bed, he finds a brand new skateboard!

Summary and Conclusion:
1. What would have happened if Johnny had read the note and obeyed it right away?
2. What if there wasn't any skateboard under the bed, should Johnny have read the note?
3. What do you think he will do the next time?
4. What will you do the next time you have an opportunity to obey?
5. Have students look up verses on obedience (Scripture list). Read and discuss them with the class.

Conclude with a prayer that God will grant all of His children obedient hearts.

Exercise Ten

· ·

Share and Care

by Paul Veit

Age: Grades 1–3

Setting: An enclosed area where you can hide treats; a follow-up to a Bible lesson

Time: 25 minutes

Goal: To help children focus on the values of sharing and compassion.

Leader Preparation: To teach the Bible stories first using flannelgraph or other visual aides; also, enough treats such as chocolate kisses for one per child hidden throughout the area; to make it more interesting for the children, blindfolds, extra t-shirts, and large rubber bands

Scripture: Matthew 20:29–34; John 6:1–13; Ephesians 4:32a

The Exercise:

The teacher tells two brief Bible stories. The first story is about the boy who shares his lunch, from John 6:1–13. This story illustrates sharing. The second story, from Matthew 20:29–34, is about two blind men who receive their sight. This story illustrates compassion. Ask the children if they understand the stories. Make sure they understand that these stories are about sharing and compassion.

1. Ask half the class to act as the blind or crippled people for the exercise. Tie blindfolds on those designated blind. For those who are crippled, use the extra-roomy t-shirts and have the kids pull their arms inside, so it looks like they are armless. Or, use big, sturdy rubber bands over their shoes to bind their feet together so they can't walk normally.
2. Explain to the "nonhandicapped" children this is their opportunity to demonstrate sharing and caring, as was discussed with the Bible stories.
3. Now, it is time to start looking for the chocolate kisses. When children find more than 1, ask them what they should do with the second 1. Encourage them to show compassion and to share with the others.
4. After they find all the kisses, take off the blindfolds, etc., and make sure every student has a treat. Talk about how a child would feel who never gets the treats that everybody else gets.

Summary and Conclusion:

1. Ask the "handicapped" children how they felt when they couldn't get to the candy.
2. Then ask how it felt when others were kind enough to share with them.
3. Ask the children who found more than one candy how it felt to give one up.
4. Which is worse, giving up a candy or watching someone else do without one?
5. Would they feel differently if they were the "handicapped" one?

To conclude, remind the children that human beings are naturally selfish and only God can give us caring, generous hearts. Encourage the children to ask God for kind and loving hearts, and pray with them about this.

Building Biblical Values

Older and Wiser

by Terry Rice

Age: Grade 5

Setting: Sunday school class

Time: 20–30 minutes

Goal: To give children an opportunity to value what adults have to offer them

Leader Preparation: Paper and drawing equipment for each student

Scripture: Leviticus 19:32; Job 12:12; Titus 2:2; Hebrews 5:14

The Exercise:
1. Think about two people who are important in your life. One must be a grown-up and the other a child about your age. They may be a teacher, parent, neighbor, uncle, friend in this class, etc.
2. Use this paper and draw a picture of both people. The drawing can be a simple stick figure like the one on the board, but make sure you show which one is an adult and which one is a child.
3. Next, make a list under each person. List all the good things that each one does for you. What do you like about them? How do they make you feel good? What can you learn from them?
4. Finally, at the bottom of your paper, write two or three sentences describing how your life would be different if this person were not around. What would happen to you if this person were missing?

Summary and Conclusion:
Children can share with the class some of the things they listed for each person and who the person is. See if a pattern emerges, comparing and contrasting what the children value in the adults they have listed with what they value in the child. Each has a value. Do the children notice that mature

adults have valuable qualities not available in children? How does valuing maturity conflict with American culture today? Can the children acknowledge how important responsible adults are in their lives?

Conclude with Scriptures about respect for older people and a prayer of gratitude for God providing older and wiser persons in our lives.

Exercise Twelve

Good Advice

by Wayne Blanchard

Age: 8–12 years old

Setting: A large area indoors or out, able to be set up with obstacles; excellent for VBS or camp

Time: 30 minutes

Goal: To let the children experience some of the feelings adults have when they must exercise authority over children

Leader Preparation: A large area with obstacles set up in advance (Indoors, you can use tables, chairs, etc.); blindfolds; be prepared to lead discussion and to share applicable Scriptures; or two Scriptures ready on posters

Scripture: Proverbs 3:5–6; 10:8, 17; 11:2; Ephesians 6:14; 1 Peter 5:1–5

The Exercise:
   A. First, divide the class into an even number of groups, about six to a group, but they can be larger or smaller if needed.
   B. Next, ask for volunteers. You'll need one volunteer for every two groups.

Remove the volunteers from the groups so they will not hear the rest of the instructions.

C. Explain the game.
1. The object of the game is for a blindfolded volunteer to walk from one end of the area to the other—where the goal is—as quickly as possible.
2. One group of students will be helping with wise advice (step up here, two steps to your left there, etc.), but the other group will hinder with false and misleading instructions, which may cause collisions along the way, or direct to the wrong destination.
3. If the volunteer walks into an obstruction, he or she needs to walk around it twice before continuing toward the goal. Also, the volunteer must figure out before it is too late which group gives good advice and which one is misleading.

D. Blindfold the volunteer, and spin him or her around several times, finally pointed in any direction.
E. Silently point to the group that is to give the bad counsel.
F. After you say "Go," both groups begin trying to direct the volunteer.
G. After this first volunteer has succeeded or failed, repeat the exercise with another volunteer and two new groups. Repeat, with new volunteers (who have been in another room) and two new groups, until you are out of time.

Summary and Conclusion:
After the game is over, assemble all the children and discuss:
1. What was this game like? How are you feeling about it?
2. Ask the blindfolded volunteers how it felt to not be able to guide themselves. How did the conflicting advice feel? How did they finally figure out who gave good or bad directions?
3. Ask those in the "good advice" groups, "Think of a real-life situations where you were trying to help someone, but he or she kept getting a lot of bad advice from others. How did you feel?"
4. Ask the bad advice group, "What did it feel like to have the power to get someone into trouble? Why do people sometimes give bad advice?"
5. Kids have lots of decisions to make every day. How do you think people who are responsible for you feel when they are trying to give you their best guidance, but all around you there is conflicting or bad advice?
6. Do you think it is easy to be a parent?

Conclude by reading selected Scriptures praying sentence prayers.

Exercise Thirteen

Things I Love to Do

Adapted from Dr. Sidney Simon, Professor in the Center for Humanistic Education, University of Massachusetts

Age: Grade 4 through Adult (this exercise can have broad application)

Setting: Group

Time: 30 minutes

Goal: To help participants see the need to clarify their values and to honestly claim some of their own values

Leader Preparation: Paper and pencils, be prepared to lead the discussion

Scripture: Matthew 6:21; 12:34; Luke 6:45

The Exercise:
   A. Ask everyone to number a piece of paper from 1–20. Then everyone, including the teacher, lists as quickly as possible, 20 things in life that each really loves to do. Stress that the list is personal and that there is no right answer about what people should like.

   B. When all have listed their twenty items, it is time to code them as part of the process of value-clarification. Here are some suggested codes:
     1. Place **$** by any item that costs more than $5.
     2. Put an **R** in front of any item that involves some risk. The risk might be physical, intellectual, or emotional.
     3. Using the code letters **F** and **M**, mark the items on your list you think your father and mother might have had on their lists if they had been asked to do this same thing when they were your age.
     4. Place either the letter **P** or the letter **A** before each item. The **P** is for things you prefer doing with people, and the **A** is for things you prefer doing alone.

5. Place a number **5** in front of any item that you think would not be on your list 5 years from now.
6. Finally, go down through your list and place near each item the **date** when you did it last.

Summary and Conclusion:

Now, the teacher says, "If you look over your lists, you can see they tell a lot about you at this time in your life. What did you learn about yourself as you followed these instructions? Please tell us some of what you learned by choosing one of these sentences and completing it.

- I learned that I . . .
- I relearned that I . . .
- I noticed that I . . .
- I was surprised to see that I . . .
- I was disappointed that I . . .
- I was pleased that I . . .
- I realized that I . . .

Leader: You must be willing to make some "I learned that I . . ." statements too. Avoid platitudes. Make every effort to be as honest and authentic as possible. Perhaps you can see just how diametrically opposed "I learned that I . . ." statements are from indoctrination. Of course, some teachers could use this exercise to get kids to give them back the party line. On the other hand, using this strategy can begin to build that lifetime search for personal meaning in all of our experiences.

Exercise Fourteen

. . . .

Vote with Your Feet

by Wayne C. Metcalf

Age: Grades 5–7

Setting: A room or an enclosed area outdoors

Time: 15–20 minutes

Goal: To help children establish standards concerning the value of truthfulness

Leader Preparation: Five banners, either on poster board or on felt; each banner contains one response: Agree, Strongly Agree, Disagree, Strongly Disagree, and Don't Know; before beginning, display a banner in each corner of the room, with "Don't Know" in the center of the room (Kids can help with this task.); a Bible and hymn books or song sheets ready for the conclusion

Scripture: Matthew 10:16; Ephesians 5:15; James 3:13

The Exercise:
Read the following story to the group, and then follow the next instructions.

A class was going to have a geography test. Students would have to locate on a map the capitals of several foreign countries. Before test day, one of the students got a copy of the test from the teacher's desk and passed it around to other members of the class. Tommy was in the class, and when the answers came to him, he had to make a decision.

Tommy's choices were:
1. Take the answers and say nothing.
2. Tell the teacher.
3. Refuse to take the answers and receive a lower grade on the test while everyone else would get an A.

Now, everyone up on your feet. It's time to vote. Show what you think by walking over to the banner that tells how you feel.

. . . .

1. Tommy should tell the teacher.

    Leader: After each vote, allow students to defend the reasons for their choice. This will allow each student to own a position and put into words the reason for taking that stand. Try to explore several possible consequences for each different vote by asking, "What could happen if Tommy does _____."
2. Take the answers and say nothing.
3. Tommy should not take the answers even though everyone else will probably get an A.

(This exercise could be expanded or repeated by coming up with other stories where a moral choice is necessary.)

Summary and Conclusion:
Read the Scriptures from Matthew 10:16, Ephesians 5:15, and James 3:13. Conclude by singing "Stand Up, Stand Up for Jesus."

Exercise Fifteen

. . . .

Learning to Share

by Dave Lynch

Age: 5–6 years old

Setting: Following a Bible lesson about sharing, for example, the story of the shared lunch of bread and fish

Time: 4–10 minutes

Goal: To help students understand why sharing is good and to demonstrate ways they can share

. . . .

Leader Preparation: Be prepared to teach a Bible story on sharing prior to doing this exercise; enough snacks ready for the entire class

Scripture: Mark 6:30–44; 1 John 3:17–18

The Exercise:

After the Bible lesson, arrange to send two of the children from the class on an errand. While they are gone, pass out snacks, so that when the two errand-runners return, everyone is eating. But there is only one serving left! (To keep this from becoming a crisis, choose your errand-runners wisely. Also, to set a tone, maintain an attitude of good-natured humor about the situation.)

1. Ask the two errand-runners who should get the last snack and why.
2. Ask the class who should get the snack and why.
3. "Try" to take a snack from one of the children who is already eating it to give to the one who has none. Who deserves the snack more, the class member or the child who ran the errand?
4. Ask the class to come up with a solution to this problem.
5. Ask about sharing the snack. Who should share?

Result: Close with cutting the remaining snack in two and "finding" two more snacks, so that those who shared end up with one and a half snacks each.

Summary and Conclusion:

During craft time, have the children draw ways that they can share or help others. Repeat the Scripture from 1 John as the children work.

Giving E.T. a Tour of Earth

by Betty Jamison

Age: Grades 5–9

Setting: Youth group

Time: 30 minutes

Goal: To help youth discover which things on earth they value, why they hold these values, and to compare their values with those of Jesus

Leader Preparation: Value Chart (p. 150) ready to hand out; be prepared with Scriptures to help discover what Jesus values

Scripture: 1 Peter 3:15b

The Exercise:
Present the following challenge to the group:
1. If a friendly person from another planet—E.T., for example—wanted to see the earth, what would you show him? There is no limit to how much money you could spend or where you could go, but you would have only three weeks in which to do it all. Make a list of up to twenty things you would show.
2. Next, ask: How would the things you choose to show him reflect what you consider valuable? Hand out the Value Chart, and encourage youth to add their own ideas to it.
3. Allow several minutes for list making.

Summary and Conclusion:

1. If the group is large, have them break up into smaller groups of four to five to compare lists.
2. Then, ask several people to share their lists.
3. Put their responses on the board. Talk about how the reason behind a certain activity reflects what sort of value we place on it (For different persons, a day at the beach could demonstrate a value of fun, beauty, exercise, or companionship).
4. Finally, have the group discuss: If Jesus were on earth today and got to show E.T. around our planet, what do you think would be on Jesus' list of top twenty items? Challenge them to back up their "Jesus list" with Scripture (For example, Matthew 6:2,19–20, 26, etc.).

Value Chart

Instructions: Circle the number you think best shows the value of each statement, with 10 being most valuable and 1 being least valuable.

1. Scientific discoveries and knowledge
   1   2   3   4   5   6   7   8   9   10

2. Cultural places, libraries, museums, theater
   1   2   3   4   5   6   7   8   9   10

3. Religions such as Christianity and other world religions
   1   2   3   4   5   6   7   8   9   10

4. Natural wonders such as the Grand Canyon or the Alps
   1   2   3   4   5   6   7   8   9   10

5. Forms of government, such as democracy and communism
   1   2   3   4   5   6   7   8   9   10

6. Homes and families
   1   2   3   4   5   6   7   8   9   10

7. Places of service like hospitals, Peace Corps, social service projects
   1   2   3   4   5   6   7   8   9   10

8. Industry and manufacturing; the world of things
   1   2   3   4   5   6   7   8   9   10

9. Material possessions
   1   2   3   4   5   6   7   8   9   10

10. People and meaningful personal relationships
    1   2   3   4   5   6   7   8   9   10

Mysterious Treasure Hunt

by Jeanne Williams

Age: Grades 4–9 (the game is set up for four teams of 3–5 students per team)

Setting: Outdoors or in a large room such a gym or fellowship hall; ideal for camp, day camp, Pioneer Club, Christian Ambassadors, Awana, etc.; probably at least two leaders necessary to guide the game; if played out in the woods or a large field, one leader could accompany each of the four groups, and the game could take longer by having more stops or more space between stops

Time: 30–45 minutes

Goal: To allow children to practice cooperating in order to learn both the difficulty and the value of cooperation (By this action participants will be acting on a value, step 6 of the 7 steps to internalize a value; and during the discussion, they will be prizing and cherishing the value of cooperation, which is step 4; see pp. 8–9)

Leader Preparation: Prepare all the components of the game: lay out the course, prepare puzzle-clues and envelopes for clues. Plan a prize or treasure for the end and have questions ready for discussion. Go over the rules of the game with all the leaders, so everyone understands how the game works.

Materials necessary: twelve envelopes and twelve 6 x 6 squares of cardstock. Use eight of these 6 x 6 cards to write out two sets of directions to each of four hiding places. On the other four cards write directions to a single place. (See example on p. 154). Now, cut each card into a puzzle of twelve pieces.

Envelope 1 will contain six pieces from card A and six pieces from card B.

Envelope 2 will contain the remaining twelve pieces.

Continue making clue cards, cutting them into puzzles, and arranging them according to the pattern of the game as displayed in the Mysterious Treasure Hunt diagram (p. 155).

Scripture: Romans 12:4–6a; 1 Corinthians 12:12, 14–27

The Exercise:
A. Explanation:

When you start the game, you will give team A envelope 1. Inside envelope 1 will be twelve puzzle pieces—six of which give the first clue team A needs to move on, and six of which give the clue team B needs. When team B opens its envelope, they will find they have twelve puzzle pieces, too—the other half of each team's first clue. Neither team A nor team B will be able to solve the mystery and find the treasure unless both teams cooperate. They must work together to assemble the puzzle pieces for each team's clue.

This is the same pattern for teams C and D. According to the Mysterious Treasure Hunt diagram, use clue cards in envelopes to send the teams around to all their different destinations. At each stopping point they will have to cooperate with a different team than before. Although the children do not know this, the final clues send all teams to the same ending place where a leader will be waiting, guarding the "treasure." Since everyone helped cooperate to get the treasure, everyone gets a part of the treasure.

One last rule adds interest to this game. None of the children is allowed to talk once the game begins. They must solve their puzzles without words.
B. Method:
1. Take the children to the starting point. Divide them into four teams and name the teams A, B, C, and D. Tell them, "We are going to play a game in which we will have to cooperate. Does anyone know what cooperate means?" Allow children to respond. "That's right, cooperation means to work together to get something done. Today, we have a treasure waiting for you, but you can only find the treasure if you can solve the mystery about where it is. To solve the mystery, you will need some good clues.
2. "I will give each team an envelope with your clue in it. But your clues are going to be all cut up into puzzle pieces! When you put the puzzle together, it will tell you where to go next. Now, here's the challenge! You will need to do a great job of cooperating in order to assemble your puzzle, because you will have only half of your puzzle pieces and the other team will have the other half.
3. "When you figure out your first puzzle-clue, take it with you to where you have to go and look in the new place for another envelope. You will find a different team there, and you will have to cooperate all over again in order to get your next treasure clue.

4. "Finally, following all the clues will lead your team to the treasure.
5. "Now, before you start, there is one very important rule: Once I hand out your team envelopes, NO ONE is allowed to talk or whisper!—not even to your own teammates! Anyone who whispers will have to leave the game and go over to the 'Jail' until the game is over."
6. Leader now hands out the first puzzle-clue envelope to each team and tells them to open them. The leaders watch the children to help them remember not to talk, and one leader should be near the treasure by the time the children are about to discover it.

   Note: The treasure can be as simple or as elaborate as the occasion demands. For a really big treat, have a piñata stuffed with candies that the children can take turns trying to knock down. Something as simple as enough sticks of sugarless gum for each student also constitutes a satisfying reward. Nonfood treasure could be small trinkets, similar to party favors.

   Before you distribute the treasure, first lead the group discussion. (Children will pay attention better if the treat is still ahead.)

Summary and Conclusion:

Summarize with a discussion. Return any "prisoners" from "jail" to the group. Have children sit in a circle, and ask the following questions:
1. How did you feel about not being able to talk? Was it hard?
2. Do you feel like you cooperated during the game? What was hard about that? What was easier?
3. Could you have found the treasure without cooperating?
4. Ask the children to share with the group specific instances in which one cooperated with another individual.
5. What were some times when you might have finished faster if you could have cooperated better?
6. What are some times in real life when it's important to cooperate?
7. Why, do you think, do some people not want to cooperate?
8. Have each child think of 1 area in the coming week where he or she can be a better cooperator.

Conclude by reading selected verses from Romans 12:4–6a or 1 Corinthians 12:12, 14–27, preferably using a *Good News* or *Living Bible*. Then distribute the treasure.

Exercises for Children 153

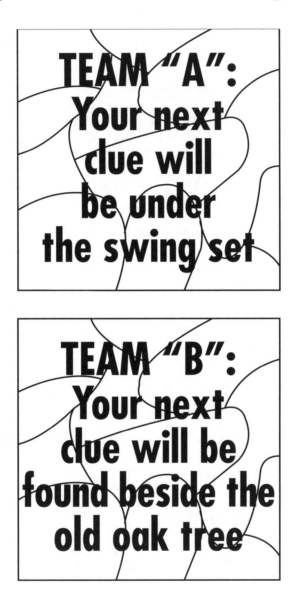

Envelope 1 will contain six pieces from card A and six pieces from card B. Envelope 2 will contain the remaining twelve pieces.

Mysterious Treasure Hunt

This diagram is to assist in explaining the rules of "Treasure Hunt." The tree, swing set, tree stump, gate, and door are only hypothetical points. Any easily described places, indoors or outdoors, where an envelope could be hidden would do fine.

Key:

(A)	= Team A
E-1	= Envelope 1
– – –	= Lines of movement
<—>	= Lines of movement

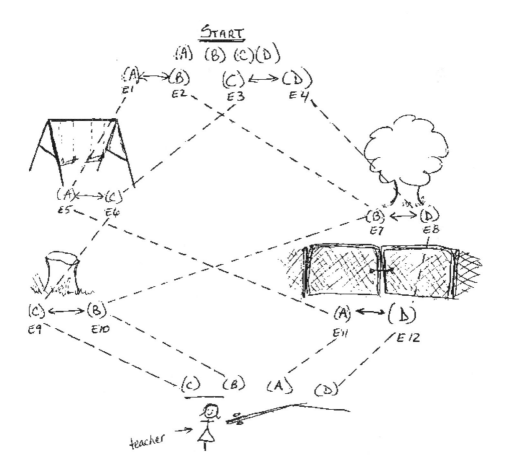

Exercise Eighteen

Climb to the Top

by Dan Dunn

Age: Grades 1–5

Setting: For individual assessment or as part of a small group while children are coloring or playing with Play-Doh® or Legos®

Time: 20–30 minutes

Goal: To discover which level (according to Kohlberg's classification, appendix 1) the children are on; to provide an opportunity to nudge them on to a higher level by the wise use of questions (Values that will be addressed include: honesty, promptness, kindness, sensitivity, compassion, and obedience)

Leader Preparation: In advance on a large poster, draw a pyramid (see illustration, p. 157) divided into boxes numbered 1 to 7. Borrowing from other games, have ready for each child a distinctive marker (for example, use colored chips or different-shaped small objects from a board game). Review Kohlberg's levels (appendix 1) and the sorts of questions that free people up to examine their values without becoming defensive (appendix 3).

Scripture: Proverbs 20:11

The Exercise:
The goal of the game is for each child to start at box 1 and progress through 7. The children mark their progress with the items listed above. Children move ahead by answering the question that has the same number as the box. Children may take turns, but each child's answer must be his or her own.
1. Your parents told you to pick up your room before you left for school. You forgot to do your homework yesterday, and you only have about 20 minutes before the bus comes. What should you do?
2. You get on the bus for school. Later on, a friend of yours also gets

on the bus. This friend does not sit with you. It is a rule not to leave your seat on the bus. Would you go sit with your friend?

3.   When you get to school, the teacher introduces a new student to the class. This new student does not have any friends, and you are very popular. Later, the class divides up into reading groups of three. You and a good friend start a group. For the third person, should you invite another friend or the new kid?

4.   Recess comes, and the class decides to play kickball. The smallest kid in the class ends up on the other team. Every time this kid is up, he/she makes an out. Now your team is way ahead, and this kid is up to kick the ball. The ball comes your way. Do you put the kid out or let him/her reach first?

5.   At lunch, the woman in the lunch line forgets to punch your ticket. This means you get a free lunch. What should you do?

6.   Today, the teacher lets you out of school early. Your mother always tells you should come right home after school. You go by the playground, and you wonder about playing for a little while. What do you do?

7.   Your (brother or sister) takes cookies out of the cookie jar after school. After dinner your mom goes to the jar to give you some cookies for dessert. Then, she notices the cookies are almost gone. Your mom asks you both who took the cookies. Your (brother or sister) doesn't say anything. What should you say?

Summary and Conclusion:

Tell the children that not all of these questions are easy ones to answer, and sometimes people struggle with what's right and wrong. Invite them to discuss things like this with a parent or a Sunday school teacher who knows the Bible and who can help them think about choices and consequences.

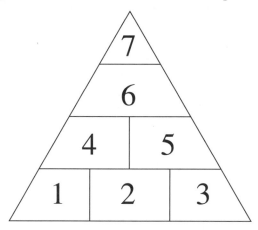

Exercise Nineteen

"I Like to . . ."

by Carolyn Tunnell

Age: 5–9 years old

Setting: Group of 10–12

Time: 45 minutes

Goal: To motivate children toward good use of leisure time

Leader Preparation: Scissors, large poster paper (prepared as described below), felt-tip marking pens, magazines, and glue

Scripture: 1 Timothy 6:17b: "God gives us richly all things to enjoy."

The Exercise:
  A. Have one big poster with three divisions or three smaller posters. The headings should be: (1) I like to participate in . . . , (2) I like to watch or listen to . . . , and (3) I would like a chance to . . . Make headings in large print with a marker, but leave lots of space underneath for the items the children will cut from the magazines.
  B. As the children find things they want to put on the poster, help them sort out the difference between lively activities (such as sports, games, projects, taking care of pets) and passive activities (watching TV or listening to the stereo or the radio).
  C. Encourage the children to stretch their imaginations and find unusual, creative things that they would like a chance to do (build a tree house, take a rocket to the moon, have a backyard circus). If you can't find a picture for the unusual idea, sketch the idea onto the poster with markers.
  D. When all of the children have been able to find pictures of several things they like or would like to do and have glued them to the poster, assemble them as a group to brainstorm about the creative use of leisure time.

E. In addition to things that have come up while doing the poster, you could include some of the following questions:
   1. Why do we have leisure?
   2. Is it ever OK to just do nothing? Why or why not?
   3. Are some things we do with our spare time better than others? Why?
   4. Do the better leisure activities usually cost more money? If this seems to be true, is there something we can do about it?
   5. Are some of the things that we would like to do impossible? Why?
   6. Have the children evaluate how they use or develop skills in the different activities.
   7. Talk about how a good mind, a healthy body, good friends, and creative imagination contribute to leisure time.

Summary and Conclusion:

Of the things they would like to do but never have, help the children explore any realistic possibilities. If a child identifies such an area, the leader could follow up with parents to see if they are receptive to expanding opportunities for new activities with their child.

Exercise Twenty

Swiss Family Robinson Adventure

by Gerald Jackson

Age: Children (this exercise can have broad application)

Setting: A family time, to be done during an evening; could also be adapted to an outdoor camp setting, or used in a classroom in a Christian school where the teacher has been reading the chosen book to the children during story time

Time: About 30 minutes (once the meal is over and the exercise begins)

Goal: To introduce children to the concept of a value system including starting to understand how they determine values, what is valuable to them, and what they value in others

Leader Preparation: This exercise is built around the survival/adventure theme found in *Robinson Crusoe* or *Swiss Family Robinson*. At home or at school the leader can read a bit of the story to the children over several days or weeks. At camp, one of the leaders should be familiar enough with whichever story to be able to summarize it for the children. Also at home or at camp, the supper menu could reflect the desert island theme with the kids helping to decorate and set the mood.

Scripture: Proverbs 12:11; 31:10; Ecclesiastes 4:6; 5:10; 10:18; Matthew 6:21; Mark 8:36

The Exercise:
   A. After supper in the desert island setting, the family should gather in a comfortable spot. Briefly discuss the story and ask the children what things the people who were stranded on an island valued the most.

B. Next, ask the children to go to their rooms for 10 minutes with this question in mind: "If a tornado or fire were about to destroy your home and all your possessions, what would you most want to save?" (If in a classroom, give the children several minutes to list the items they would choose.)

C. When the children reassemble, each should have with them what they value most of their possessions. Let people, one person at a time, tell why they picked the items they did. Why is it valuable?

D. Some questions:
   1. What did you learn you could do without?
   2. What was the hardest thing to leave behind? Why?
   3. Did the things you chose cost a lot of money?
   4. Did anyone choose money? Why or why not?

E. Discuss the value of a good mind, a healthy body, good friends, the power of imagination and creativity, etc.

Summary and Conclusion:
Conclude by challenging the children to explain this statement: There are people who know the cost of everything and the value of nothing.

Exercise Twenty-One

. . . .

Build a Bridge

Age: Elementary through Junior High

Setting: Groups of about 4–10, indoors or outdoors

Time: About 30 minutes

. . . .

Goal: To challenge the children to work as a group and to choose and prize the value of cooperation

Leader Preparation: Markers, concrete blocks, and boards of various lengths; at least two adults

Scripture: Romans 12:1–18; Philippians 2:1–2; 4:1–3

The Exercise:
1. The challenge the children face is to construct a "bridge" across a "river" out of the materials available. Indoors you can designate the river with masking tape on the floor. Outdoors, try mowing a wide-enough path through taller grass. Naturally, there is a prize on the other side.
2. Have available a few concrete blocks and some boards. One board should be long enough to cross the "river." Let other boards be half as long or almost long enough, and have a few boards that are too short to do much of anything with.
3. To make the game more challenging and interesting for the older children, you can use the following variations:
   • Use blindfolds and make everyone "blind" except one person.
   • Using masking tape, mark arms or legs on some of the children as "broken" and unable to be used.
4. Anyone who falls into the "river" drowns and is out of the game.
5. Now, the leader stands back and lets the children go to work. Different groups of children demonstrate a huge variety of responses in how spontaneously and how effectively they will cooperate to build a bridge. The leader should only intervene if life or limb is about to be endangered.
6. If at the end of 15 minutes the bridge still isn't done, the leader calls time.

Summary and Conclusion:
Conclude with a prize and a group discussion. (On a hot day outdoors, the prize can be cups of cold juice or popsicles.) Depending upon their experiences with the task, discussion will vary with different groups, but here are issues to address:
1. How did each child feel about the initial challenge?
2. Was the exercise fun, or not?
3. If it was or wasn't any fun, did that have anything to do with how well they worked as a team?
4. Is there anything anyone would like to do differently next time?
5. If the group had a hard time cooperating, are there feelings to be aired or conflicts to settle?

6. Finally, ask the children what they have learned today and especially if they have learned anything about working together as a group.

Select one of the Scriptures in a readable translation to share with the group.

[With gratitude for this idea to my friend, Ron Cox]

Exercise Twenty-Two

Hero Selection

by Beth Brown

Age: Grades 1–3 (can be adapted for older preschoolers)

Setting: Group of children: Sunday school, VBS, Pioneer Club

Time: 10–25 minutes (depends upon age of group)

Goal: To equip students to bridge the gap between values displayed by Bible heroes and the value of their own obedience in everyday life.

Leader Preparation: Pictures of Bible heroes, labeled; chalkboard or large paper to write on; Bible

Scripture: 1 Corinthians 10:11; Hebrews 6:12

The Exercise:
A. Leader arranges pictures of Adam, Noah, Abraham, Moses, Joseph, Joshua, David, and Daniel for children to see, and asks, "Which of these people would you most like to be like?"
(For preschoolers, limit choices to three or four heroes that they have recently studied, and talk about each one briefly to remind the children what each was like.)

B. To stimulate discussion:
   1. Why did you most want to be like_____?
   2. Did anyone choose another hero? Why?
   3. What are some ways we want to be like these people?
   4. What does *obedience* mean? Were these people obedient?
   5. Does God ask *us* to do things, too? What things might be the same? Different?
   6. What happens if we don't obey God? What happens if we do?
   7. What are some things that you know God likes you to do?
   8. What 1 special thing would God like you to do today?
   9. Make a definite plan about how and when you will do it.

Summary and Conclusion:
   Leader concludes by reading one of the Bible verses in an easy-to-understand version.

Exercise Twenty-Three

· ·

Prejudice and Partiality

by Sue Kroeta

Age: Elementary through Junior High

Setting: A reasonably consistent group from session to session, with 10–30 participants

Time: Two consecutive classroom periods (50 minutes each), allowing time for a 10–15 minute discussion at the end of the second class

· ·

Goal: To experience and to talk about the feelings that occur when they are oppressed and when they oppress others; as a result, they will better understand the dynamics of prejudice and the worth of seeing all people as equal before God (Students should proceed from the self-interest of Kohlberg's stage 2 to the concern for social awareness of stage 3; see appendix 1)

Leader Preparation: Understand the game, maintain a playful attitude, and be prepared to lead discussion and apply the Scriptures at the end

Scripture: Acts 10:34–35; James 2:1–4, 8–9

The Exercise:
   A. Introduce the exercise to the students as a game to help them learn more about how it feels to be considered different. It will be important for teachers to maintain a playful attitude with all the children as they carry out this experiment.
   B. On the first day, the instructor will define the rules:
      1. All children with blue eyes will be recognized with special privileges, such as sitting close to the teacher, being given more positive attention, first to eat the snack, etc.
      2. All children with brown eyes will be given lesser privileges, such as sitting away from the teacher, more negative attention (stress their faults), last to eat snacks, etc.
      3. The teacher will make a big deal of saying how wonderful the blue-eyed kids are because of their blue eyes and pointing out flaws with the brown-eyed children and saying it is a result of having brown eyes.
      4. Blue-eyed children may not play with brown-eyed children.
      5. Brown-eyed children must wear a special label, such as a colored tag pinned to their shirts.
      6. All this goes on as the students go through a regular class session.
   C. To begin the second class session, the teacher announces that the tables are turned. Brown-eyed children will now become the favored ones, and all the rules of the previous session are reversed. Allow the class to proceed under the new rules until discussion time (allow 10–15 minutes at the end of the class).

Summary and Conclusion:
    To begin discussion, the teacher will tell the children to throw away the special identifying tags pinned to their shirts, because there will be no more differences between being blue-eyed and brown-eyed people.

Questions for discussion:
1. How did it feel to be separated and made to feel different?
2. How did you feel when your group was favored?
3. How did you feel when your group was treated poorly?
4. Teacher, take a moment to talk about changes you observed in the behavior or personalities of the children between the two class periods.
5. Was this arrangement fair on either day?
6. No one can help having the eye color God gave him or her—it's not a choice. What if the differences in treatment had been a result of something we can choose, like doing homework or following the rules?
7. (Especially for adolescents) Sometimes people *like* to separate themselves into groups and have a rivalry (e.g., sports). What is the difference between that and what happened in class?
8. What do we call it when someone treats you unfairly because of something you have no control over? (prejudice)
9. Can you think of groups that experience prejudice? Name some.
10. Now that you know how it feels to receive prejudice, what difference will it make in how you feel about others? How you treat others?
11. Do we know how God feels about these things? Let's look it up in the Bible: James 2:1–4, 8–9; Acts 10:34–35.
12. Conclude with a prayer that God will give us eyes to see all people the way He does.

Follow-up:
One or 2 weeks later, discuss the lesson and talk about ways to apply what the children have learned.

Right or Wrong Game

by Pam Welp

Age: Elementary

Setting: Group(s) of 4 children

Time: 30 minutes

Goal: To stimulate children to identify right and wrong acts and to identify their own feelings when they do similar acts

Leader Preparation: For each group of 4 children, make a board on 12" x 18" construction paper made according to the pattern on page 168, and a set of cards with the following sentences:

- I broke my brother's toys.
- I called my sister names.
- I talked back to Mom.
- I did not clean up my toys when Mom asked.
- I stole a piece of gum at the candy counter.
- I cut in the front of the lunch line.
- I lied to Dad about using his tools and not returning them.
- I cheated on a math assignment.
- I wrote on a library book.
- I grabbed a toy from a friend.
- I got in a fight on the playground.
- I helped Mom clean up after dinner.
- I shared my bike with my friend.
- I helped a kid who fell and hurt his leg.
- I cleaned up my room.
- I went to bed when asked.
- I helped Mom take care of the baby.
- I shared my things with someone who does not have much.

- I helped Dad water the plants.
- I made a card for someone who was sick.
- I did my homework without a reminder.
- I stuck up for a kid that others were teasing.

Mix these cards up and lay them face down next to the board. You will also need one die, a penny, a nickel, a dime, and a quarter.

Scripture: Proverbs 20:11

The Exercise:
1. Divide children into groups of 4, with game equipment for each group, and let each participant choose the coin he or she wants.
2. The one with the penny (or whatever coin leader chooses) starts by rolling the die and moving his or her coin along the board the number of spaces on the die.
3. When players land on a square with an **X**, they choose a card and read the sentence aloud. (Early grades may need some assistance to read the cards.) Then they must say whether it was a right or wrong thing to do and give the reason for their answer.
4. If the answer is "right," then they move ahead one space. If the answer is "wrong," they move back one space.
5. The game continues with everyone taking turns until everyone reaches the happy face.

Summary and Conclusion:
1. Have you ever done any of the things that were written on the cards?
2. How did you feel after you did those things?
3. Do you feel more happy after you do good things or bad things?
4. What is something you can do today that will make you feel happy?

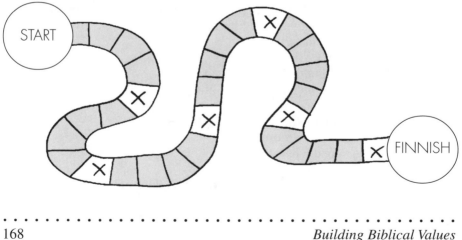

The Shared Lunch

by Lorrie Metzger

Age: Grades 1–5

Setting: Any group of children

Time: About 30 minutes

Goal: To help children experience the value of sharing, either by participating or because of not participating

Leader Preparation: Be prepared to tell the Bible story using a flannelgraph; enough paper and crayons for each child and a Bible

Scripture: John 6:1–13

The Exercise:
1. Using the flannelgraph, tell the story of the boy who shared his lunch of loaves and fishes. Note the boy's willingness to share, the miraculous results, and what might have happened if he had not shared.
2. Give each child one sheet of paper and one crayon, using as many colors as possible. Tell the children to draw a picture either of the Bible story or of a time when they shared something they had with someone else. You might suggest that the pictures would be more interesting if more colors are used.
3. Give each child an opportunity to explain his or her picture.
4. Leader discusses what they observed. If the children shared the crayons, discuss how much more interesting the pictures are when many colors are used. If they did not share crayons, discuss what a difference it would have made in their pictures if they had shared.

Summary and Conclusion:
Leader wraps up with a discussion of the following:
1. Was it hard to give away your crayon? Why or why not?
2. Do you think the boy in the story was afraid of going hungry if he gave away his lunch?
3. Would you have given away your lunch? Why or why not?
4. Did you have to ask for a different crayon, or did someone just give it to you? Which is better?
5. Do you like your picture better with 1 or many colors? Why?
6. Is sharing what we have similar to making a picture with many colors? How?
7. What are some things we can share with others?

Exercise Twenty-Six

Time, Talent, and Treasure

by George Wiedman

Age: 8–10 years old

Setting: 3 large tables with chairs for the children to work at

Time: 45 minutes

Goals: To expand the children's ideas of ways to give to others

Leader Preparation: A teacher for each table; the tables spaced apart from each other; Bibles, song books, construction paper, and markers or crayons;

three signs: time, talent, treasure; information about nursing homes that would appreciate a visit or individuals who are ill

Scripture: Matthew 14:15–21 (feeding of the 5,000); Mark 10:46–52 (blind man); Acts 9:36 (Dorcas)

The Exercise:

Put a different sign on each table, so you have one designated for time, one for talent, and one for treasure. Divide the class into 3 groups and send each group to a different table. After 15 minutes, the children will rotate to a different table, until each group has been to each table.

At the table labeled **time,** teach the children the story of Jesus and the blind man. Show the class how Jesus took time out of His busy schedule to help someone. Begin organizing a class trip to a nursing home. Encourage children to give their time to go and visit an elderly person. Teach them a song they can sing when they get there.

At the table labeled **talents,** teach the story of Dorcas from the book of Acts. Show how Dorcas made clothes for the people in her town. Using the construction paper, have the children make get-well cards for all of the sick people in the church or in the neighborhood. If you are aware of specific individuals who are ill, talk about them so the children can picture who they are.

At the **treasure** table, teach the story of the feeding of the 5,000. Show how the young boy gave his lunch to Jesus. Tell the children that next week there is going to be a missionary box in the classroom. Encourage children to bring something of theirs (not money) to give children overseas. Talk about what children overseas might appreciate.

At the end of the 45 minutes, each child will have been exposed to giving in three areas: time, ability, and possessions and will have concrete opportunities to practice each type of giving.

Summary and Conclusion:

Remind childeren to bring donation for next week and to save the date of the nursing home visit. Encourage them to look for ways to use their time, talent, and treasure at home and at shool.

Exercise Twenty-Seven

Wonderfully Made

by Holly Faler

Age: Children

Setting: Groups at camp or any informal setting

Time: 20–30 minutes

Goal: To foster awareness of the world around them, to give practice in making group decisions, to encourage respect for their own uniqueness and the uniqueness of others

Leader Preparation: Paper bags, Psalm 139:14 written out on a large card

Scripture: Psalm 139:14

The Exercise:
1. Assign children to form groups of 2 or 3, and give each group a small paper bag.
2. Ask them to pick out 2 similar objects from nature (without destroying anything), such as 2 rocks, 2 twigs, or 2 flowers. They must decide as a group what object to bring back and which 2 specific examples of that object to bring back.
3. When they return, have them sit in a circle with their group and quietly pull out what they have in their bags.
4. Have them look at the objects and see how even though they are the same thing (e.g., rocks) they are not exactly alike. Ask them if they agree with this statement.
5. Leader says, "You are all children with legs and arms and a head that has eyes, ears, nose, mouth, and hair, but God gave us each something special to make us a little different from everyone else. God chose to make everybody different because He likes differences, just like He made each flower and rock a little bit different."

6. For discussion:
    Have you noticed how everyone is different?
    Are we always pleased about our differences?
    How could we appreciate or enjoy differences between people?
7. Leader displays the card with Psalm 139:14 written on it and everyone reads it out loud. Help the children practice so that they can memorize the verse, or portions of it.

Summary and Conclusion:
Ask the children to bow their heads and think of one way God has made them unique that they will praise Him for. Allow time for silent prayer, then close with a general prayer praising God for all the wonderful and different things He has made—especially people.

Exercise Twenty-Eight

Golden Rule

by Chuck Orwiler

Age: Grades 1–3

Setting: Groups of students in Sunday school or after-school clubs

Time: 60 minutes

Goal: For children to memorize Matthew 7:12, to observe an example of its application, to encourage empathy with one another, and to choose a specific application in their own lives

Leader Preparation: Arrange for several children to bring interesting, attractive toys to share; 2 hand puppets; drawing materials for each class member; a blackboard and a Bible

Scripture: Matthew 7:12

The Exercise:
1. Spend the first 10 minutes trading special toys, showing them off, and enjoying them.
2. Ask if there are any children who want to tell the whole class about their favorite toy.
3. Using hand puppets, demonstrate a situation where two children, John and Mary, are playing with John's toy. Mary wants to play with it and John reluctantly gives it up. He tells Mary to be very, very careful. After playing for a while, Mary says, "Oh, no! I broke your favorite toy!"
4. *Leader:* "What do you think John is going to say to Mary?" Have volunteers come up, put a hand in the puppet, and say something to Mary.
5. "What do you think Mary would like to say to John?" Again, have volunteers come up.
6. Go around the class and ask the girls to finish the sentence, "I think John feels . . ." List their answers on the board. Go around the class and ask the boys, "I think Mary feels . . ." Put their answers on the board. Then ask the class if anyone wants to add anything.
7. Pass around drawing materials and have the class draw pictures of John and Mary playing together. Draw "balloons" with the words they are saying to each other.
8. Introduce the Scripture verse by reading it out of the Bible and writing it on the board or poster. Recite the verse several times as a group and then have the children copy it on the back of their art paper. (Younger children will need assistance.)
9. Back to the puppets. The next day Mary comes over to play with John again. Who wants to be Mary? And John? Let the volunteers act out the scene. Then let another pair try.
10. Explore why John should let Mary play. Incorporate both the Golden Rule and empathy on John's part. Will it be easy for him to forgive? To share? Will he be glad he did? Why?
11. *Leader:* "Think of a person who needs your kindness this week. Write their name on your paper and draw a picture of what you can do."

Summary and Conclusion:
Review the verse. Pray for each child whose name is on the papers with a unison prayer, "Jesus, help me remember to be kind to _____ this week."

Exercises for Adults
· ·

Exercise One

· ·

The Missionary Résumé

by Tom Stoner

Age: Adult

Setting: Mission societies and committees, adult classes, leadership training

Time: About 60 minutes

Goal: To teach the value of humility and dependence upon God when seeking to evaluate candidates for church positions

Leader Preparation: Enough copies of the materials so that each participant can have a copy of the following: Missionary Résumé (p. 178), Profile of a Missionary Applicant by an Interested Party (p. 179), Evaluation Questionnaire for A and B (p. 177–78), and 3 copies each of the Missionary Rating Sheet (p. 180)

Scripture: John 8:15a; 1 Corinthians 4:1–5, 6:2–5, 11:31; Zechariah 7:9; 1 Samuel 16:7b

The Exercise:
1. Distribute all the materials to the group members.
2. Instruct them to fill out two rating sheets—one for each applicant. (Allow about 10–15 minutes for this part of the exercise.)
3. Now ask them to turn to the Evaluation Questionnaire for A and B and to fill that out, also.
4. Allow time for various participants to briefly express their answers so far.

   Inform the class that both the résumé and the "Profile" are about the same applicant. Also explain that while this person received numerous positive recommendations from evangelicals, the applicant also had some extremely negative evaluations from some individuals.

· ·

Now ask the group to use the third rating sheet to evaluate this person, incorporating all the various evidences.

Summary and Conclusion:
To conclude, lead a discussion using the following questions:
1. How did balancing the two affect your first impression of the candidate submitting the résumé?
2. How did balancing the two affect your first impression of the applicant discussed in the profile?
3. Have you ever experienced something like this in real life when trying to evaluate a person or a situation?
4. What principles motivated your assessment of the applicant's inner character in each of these three samples?
5. Do you want others to judge you on first impressions? On your outward appearance? Why? Can others know what is in your heart? How?
6. What principles will guide us best when we must make evaluations? (Here, you may refer to the Scriptures listed or to other Scriptures familiar to you.)
7. Do you think you would want this person to be a pastor in our church?
8. Does this person sound familiar? Who is he?
      (Both applicant documents were taken from biblical information on the apostle Paul.)

Evaluation Questionnaire for A and B

A is the candidate in the Résumé
B is the candidate from the Profile

1. What objective evidence do you have that reveals the inner character of each person?
   A. _____
   B. _____

2. How do you feel about the applicants, not having met them?
   A. _____
   B. _____

3. What kind of an example is each man to his church people?
   A. _____
   B. _____

. . . .

4. How well could you relate to each person?
   A. _____
   B. _____

5. How accurately does either document reveal the "real" person?
   A. _____
   B. _____

Missionary Résumé

Dear Foreign Missionary Board:

I grew up a devout follower of Judaism, having been raised in an orthodox Jewish family. My parents taught me much of the Hebrew Bible, and I studied to become a rabbi. When the Jews for Jesus movement began to gain popularity, I began to crusade to keep Jewish youth faithful to the belief of our fathers. I traveled the country, much in demand as a speaker, and I stirred up much resentment toward the Christians from faithful Jews and Gentiles alike, shutting down many Jews for Jesus activities. My eloquence in debating enabled me to humiliate Christians on a number of occasions.

While traveling to such a speaking engagement, I accepted Christ as my Savior as a result of a vision of Christ that I received. I then had several other ecstatic experiences with God. I have since then dedicated my life to proclaiming Christ. I have felt a real burden for my own people and have sought to evangelize them at every opportunity. I have led hundreds of people to Christ and have seen them stand firm in the faith.

I have been active in church planting, founding over ten churches in major metropolitan areas. These churches have had a large number of Jewish people in them for the most part. My training for this work has been through a discipleship program with a recognized leader in church missions among Jewish people.

I have traveled extensively, engaged in personal evangelism constantly, been unceasing in discipling men in the faith, preached frequently, taught in many churches, raised funds for poor believers, kept in touch with my converts by mail, spent much time in prayer and fasting, and have had great concern for the churches I started.

I have learned to endure all types of adversity, such as lack of finances, persecution from Jews, and going hungry. Because of my perseverance and my unfaltering faithfulness to Jesus Christ through all of these things, I believe I can ably fulfill all the duties of a missionary under your board.

I have a close walk with the Lord and receive much guidance directly from Him. Enclosed are numerous recommendations from well-known Christians in several different churches and parachurch agencies with which I have served in the Lord's cause.

In Christ,
Missionary Applicant

Profile of a Missionary Applicant by an Interested Party

- Converted as an adult with no Christian upbringing.

- Educated himself by self-study for several years before getting involved in a church.

- Once he joined a church, he began immediately to take leadership positions.

- Has had heated arguments with other church leaders over both polity and personnel, once splitting a missionary effort.

- After beginning church work, he has moved frequently; the longest stay at one church was three years. He stayed at other churches only a few weeks, often under questionable circumstances.

- Antagonizes non-Christians by uncouth public evangelism methods, resulting in several threats on his life.

- Has not sought further formal study and has no degree from any recognized evangelical institution.

- His church services run way over their allotted times.

- Is unmarried and seems to be somewhat of a male chauvinist.

- Has a record of poor health himself, being frequently ill, and is unable to sleep well. He seems to pick associates who also have recurring health problems.

- Has a record of being in and out of jail for disturbing the peace while preaching in public places.

- He has repeatedly disagreed with noted leaders of the church concerning his future plans, and he exhibits unconciliatory behavior.

- He claims to have direct communications from God and to have God's truth to every problem which he hears of.

- He does have a record of success in recording numerous decisions for Christ, but doesn't often stay long enough to follow up the people he has led to the Lord.

Missionary Rating Sheet

Instructions: Rate the applicant according to the following 5-point scale, placing an *X* in the appropriate space.

	Excellent	Good	Average	Poor	Terrible	
Modest						Proud
	5	4	3	2	1	
Objective						Subjective
	5	4	3	2	1	
Dedicated						Half-hearted
	5	4	3	2	1	
Good Reputation						Poor Reputation
	5	4	3	2	1	
Amiable						Alienates People
	5	4	3	2	1	
Loving						Cold, Indifferent
	5	4	3	2	1	
Disciplined						Undisciplined
	5	4	3	2	1	
Hard Working						Lazy
	5	4	3	2	1	
Secure						Insecure
	5	4	3	2	1	
Sensitive						Insensitive
	5	4	3	2	1	
Good chance of success in ministry						Poor chance of success in ministry
	5	4	3	2	1	

Values in Church Life

by Bob Cook

Age: Adult (especially persons in church leadership)

Setting: Groups on planning retreats, board meetings, or training sessions

Time: 45–60 minutes

Goal: To encourage leaders to contrast, in a practical fashion, their ideal church priorities with what actually uses up most of the time and resources in their own local church

Leader Preparation: A copy of the Church Values Survey (p. 182) for each participant; questions to stimulate group discussion; Bibles and concordances for reference

Scripture: Matthew 6:33; Ephesians 4:1–16; 1 and 2 Timothy; Titus

The Exercise:
1. Each participant receives a copy of the Church Values Survey.
2. In the first column, prioritize the items according to their importance as *you* see it. The most urgent should be number 1, and the least urgent number 12. Also, make a note of any items you feel are important that are not on this list. Complete column 1 in full before going to column 2.
3. In the second column, rank these same items according to the amount of attention they receive in your local church. Most attention gets number 1, least attention gets number 12.

Summary and Conclusion:
1. Compare your two lists. How are they different? Why are they different? Should they be the same? What changes need to be made on which list? Which Scriptures come to mind as you think about these issues?

Exercises for Adults

2. After time for individual thought, have the group compare answers and discuss the issues raised. Encourage participants to back up their positions with Scriptures. Have concordances available.

Church Values Survey

Directions: As you can see, there are 12 statements and after each statement, there are two columns. In the first column, rank these 12 items in order of their importance as you see it. The most urgent should be 1, the least urgent, 12. Complete in full before going on to the second column.

Then in the second column, rank these same 12 items according to the amount of attention they receive in your local church. The one that actually gets the most attention you should mark 1, least attention, 12.

		Column 1	Column 2
1.	Raising money and spending it	___	___
2.	Developing the music program of the church	___	___
3.	Getting workers to fill all the jobs in the church	___	___
4.	Spiritual growth of all members, enabling them to become mature in faith	___	___
5.	Winning local people to Christ	___	___
6.	Building and maintaining larger and more attractive church buildings	___	___
7.	Maintaining or building church attendance	___	___
8.	Helping to relieve starvation and suffering in famine areas of the world	___	___
9.	Foreign missionary work	___	___
10.	Helping to relieve poverty and racial prejudice in the local community	___	___
11.	Keeping the programs that already exist functioning in the church	___	___
12.	Developing a sense of fellowship, love, and mutual concern	___	___

Death on the Bridge

by Roger Coombs

Age: Adult and Youth

Setting: Group

Time: 45 minutes for the story and questions; add 15 minutes if you plan to study the "fool" Scriptures

Goal: To let participants see the value they place upon people and to deal with the concept of situational ethics

Leader Preparation: Be prepared to tell the story and to draw the attached diagram large enough so that everyone can see it; Bibles and at least one concordance

Scripture: Proverbs 10:21

The Exercise:
Draw the diagram (see p. 185) and tell this story:

Once upon a time there lived a couple (A and B) who had been married several years. A was a traveling salesperson who had to be away from home a great deal, often as much as 12–15 hours a day. B, his wife, was forced to spend many lonely hours at home. One night A and B found time to attend a cocktail party and met another man, C, a widower, who lived across the river.

C became friendly with B and began seeing her regularly. B was flattered and enjoyed the companionship while A was gone so much. She found herself falling in love with C and would cross the bridge to the other side of the river, visit C at his house, and secretly make love. Because A was very jealous, B was very careful to return home by six o'clock when A would either come home for dinner or phone from wherever he was. This kept A from knowing that B was seeing C, and the marriage stayed intact.

One day, while B was across the river at C's house, a madman, D, climbed the bridge and began shooting at people crossing the bridge, so the police blocked the bridge and would let no one cross. When B tried to return home, she found that she could not because of the crazy sniper. With six o'clock approaching, she went instead to the ferryboat, which was the only other way across the river. When she tried to board the ferry, she found she did not have the necessary $1.50 to pay the toll. She begged and pleaded with the ferryboat captain, E, and promised him she would pay the next day when she could get home and fetch the money, but E would not yield.

Then B thought of her friend, F, who lived near the ferryboat dock, who might possibly loan her the $1.50 to cross the river. F, however, knew about B's immoral conduct with C and felt she would be guilty of aiding and abetting a wicked lifestyle if she loaned B money to cross over the river.

By now, B was getting panicky, knowing A would soon be home and discover that she was gone. So, she decided to take her chances on the bridge. Despite warnings and orders to halt, she rammed her car through the police barricade and sped across the bridge. The madman was a crack shot and shot B as her car went by. She and her car plunged into the river below and she died instantly.

Questions:

1. Who was the most responsible for B's death?
2. Rate the characters in the story from "best" to "worst."
3. How could the woman's death have been prevented?
4. Which character do you most identify with?
5. Is it scriptural to rank sins? That is, is killing someone worse than committing adultery? Why or why not?
6. Since the killer is crazy, does that mean his behavior is not wrong?
7. Since the killer is crazy, does that make him less guilty? Is there a difference between being guilty and being responsible?
8. Do people ever justify sexual sin because they're crazy in love?
9. If people cannot foresee that their actions will have lethal consequences, does that make them less responsible for their choices? How about the boatman, E, or the friend, F?

Summary and Conclusion:

The natural consequence of immoral behavior is to get caught in it sooner or later. ("Be sure your sin will find you out.") Is it loving for us to bail people out of these consequences? Does God rescue us or let us learn from our mistakes?

If there is time, have the group investigate the following "fool" Scriptures: Proverbs 1:7, 32; 10:8, 10, 13, 21; 12:15; 13:20; 14:24; 17:16; 18:2; 19:20; 26:8, 11.

Diagram for Death on the Bridge

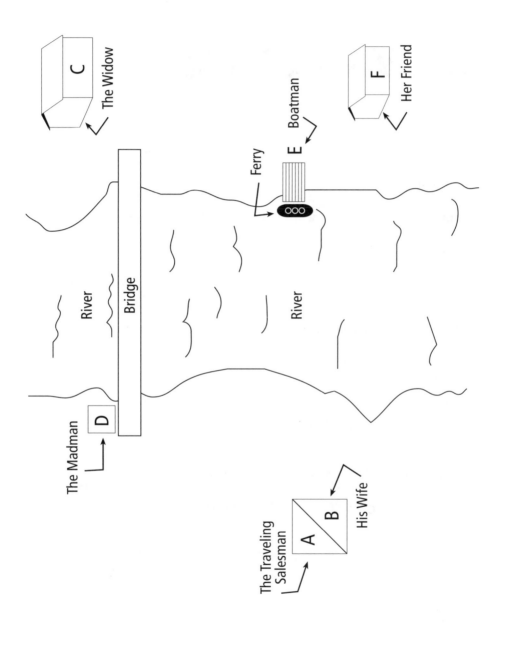

Exercise Four

....

The Work Ethic

Age: Adult and Youth

Setting: Group or one-to-one discipleship

Time: 30 minutes

Goal: To help participants think through their value structure regarding work

Leader Preparation: A Work Opinion Scale (p. 187), a pencil, and a Bible for each participant; a concordance available for looking up verses

Scripture: Genesis 2:1–3; Psalms 104:5; Proverbs 6:6; John 9:4; Philippians 4:8; Colossians 3:23

The Exercise:
Complete the Work Opinion Scale without talking to other group members.

Summary and Conclusion:
When the rating is done, as a group activity go down the list item by item, with participants explaining why they rated the items as they did. People can try to persuade each other to change their minds, and each side must defend its position with reasons. Be sure they include all the relevant Scriptures they can think of to strengthen their cases. (Hint: Use the concordance to see what the Bible says about the sluggard, rest, and work.) This should help people think through their values about work and develop more consistency between feelings and beliefs.

Work Opinion Scale

Directions: Write the number that best applies to you on the line next to the statement.

Strongly Disagree		**Indifferent**		**Strongly Agree**
1	2	3	4	5

Some Common Attitudes Toward Work and Leisure

_____ 1. Leisure is what I do after work.

_____ 2. Work is an indicator of how useful you are.

_____ 3. Work is a sign of godliness.

_____ 4. Leisure is laziness.

_____ 5. Work is what you have to do.

_____ 6. Looking after children isn't work.

_____ 7. Leisure is getting away from it all.

_____ 8. Leisure is a luxury I do not have time for.

_____ 9. Leisure is for retired old people.

_____ 10. Doing nothing is laziness.

_____ 11. Competitive sports are leisure.

_____ 12. Competitive sports are work.

_____ 13. Watching sunsets is a waste of time.

_____ 14. Art and theater are recreation.

_____ 15. Leisure is only for the rich.

_____ 16. Only oddballs have time for leisure.

_____ 17. There is no rest for the wicked.

_____ 18. Work is for slaves.

_____ 19. Intelligent people should be able to figure out how not to work.

_____ 20. We must work to be saved.

_____ 21. I work best under pressure.

_____ 22. Work is boring.

_____ 23. Going to the zoo is for kids.

_____ 24. Art is for students.

_____ 25. In all work there is profit, but mere talk leads to poverty.

Exercise Five

Nuclear Fallout

by Wayne Metcalf

Age: Adult

Setting: Group

Time: 60 minutes

Goal: To help participants establish standards concerning the value of equality

Leader Preparation: A board to list the data and the final selections where the entire group can see them and a Bible available for reference

Scripture: Romans 8:35–39

The Exercise:
  A. This is a group exercise concerning a moral dilemma that you have to solve in a limited time.
  B. *The Story:* Your group is an important government agency in Washington, D.C., in charge of experimental stations in the far outposts of civilization. Suddenly World War III breaks out. Nuclear bombs begin dropping. Places all across the world are being destroyed. People are scrambling to get into all available fallout shelters.

  Your group receives a desperate call asking for your help from one of your experimental stations. There are ten people at this station, but their fallout shelter only holds six. How can they decide which six of the ten should enter the shelter, when that means four people will be without shelter? They feel they cannot make such a momentous decision, but they have all agreed to abide by your group's decision.

  How will you decide which six can enter the shelter, realizing that the six you choose may be the only individuals who survive to start the human race over again? Your group has only twenty minutes to make the decision. Your failure to come up with a clear decision would doom all ten to death.

Due to the distances involved, none of you knows any of the ten individuals, and the information you do have is sketchy. Such as it is, here is the data:

1. Bookkeeper, male, thirty-two years old
2. His wife, six-months pregnant
3. Second-year medical student, male, black American
4. Famous historian-author, male, forty-two years old
5. Hollywood actress, sings and dances
6. Biochemist, female
7. Rabbi, fifty-four years old
8. Olympic athlete, male
9. Seminary student, female
10. Policeman with gun (they cannot be separated)

C. *Leader:* At this point, allow five minutes for each participant to think quietly and alone before starting group discussion.

D. Then, set a timer for twenty minutes and let the group discussion begin. As leader, you can lead the discussion, or you can sit back and see if one or more natural leaders will emerge—the format is your choice. But the limit of twenty minutes is firm. Emphasize to the class that some decisive action must be taken, or else all ten will perish.

Summary and Conclusion:

After the decision is made, lead a discussion of the moral reasoning various members of the group employed in order to make their choices. Possible questions could include:

1. How did it feel, having so much power over others?
2. Was this exercise fun or was it stressful? Why?
3. Have you ever heard of a similar dilemma from real life? Was it solved similarly or differently from today's dilemma?
4. What motivated the choices you ended up making?
5. How did your faith in God affect your process of making choices today?
6. Can you envision a better way to make such choices if you were one of the ten yourself? (How about drawing lots, as in the book of Jonah?)

Concluding thoughts: This is an example of a "small box." God is always larger than the box of limitations we humans can see. Although Christians are not exempt from suffering or from hard choices, prayer for a creative solution or a miracle could change the entire situation. As a group, create an ending to this story that would include a recognition of the presence of God, even in the midst of a dilemma.

Exercise Six

Resources, Policies, and the Bible

by Jane Felthauser

Age: High School through Adult

Setting: Group or one-to-one discipleship

Time: 1–2 hours

Goal: To provide participants with the elements of choosing freely, choosing from alternatives, choosing thoughtfully and reflectively, prizing and cherishing, and affirming values about dealing with poverty; elements of acting upon choices and repeating also available (see pp. 8–9)

Leader Preparation: Pencils, the written list of questions, and Bibles available for participants, and at least one concordance; a board or large paper to write on to help with group discussion

Scripture: Leviticus 25:8–37

The Exercise:
  A. Have the group read the Bible passage aloud. If there is more than one translation in the group, have them share the different nuances available for different parts of the passage.
  B. Allow some time for individuals to consider the following questions from two perspectives: (1) their personal response, and (2) in the light of the passage from Leviticus.
     1. What do you think of the welfare system?
     2. Should the poor receive public aid?
     3. Do you see any alternative?
     4. Whom do you feel a responsibility to help?

5. Should there be laws to protect the poor from high interest on loans? (What verse relates to this topic?)
6. Should there be a limit to how much a business can charge for what it sells? Should there be a limit to the percent of profit a business can make on its wares? If your answer is yes, what should be the maximum percentage of profit?
7. What percentage profit do you think God would consider just? What Scriptures do you base this opinion on? If your answer is "no," on what Scriptures do you base your opinion?
8. Should the amount you charge others for the things you sell (goods and services) be related to the amount of work done, or should you charge as much as you can possibly get? Do you see any verses that relate to this question? (See vv. 16–17.)
9. How do you regard it your right to own your possessions? How does God look at your possessions?
10. Do you feel obligated to help relatives in need? (See vs. 25.)

C. Now, lead a group discussion using the following questions. Encourage each participant to take a stand or make a statement about each item. Use the board and keep a tally of the various positions espoused.
1. What legal process did God command for establishing equality and justice among His people? Why?
2. What kinds of laws could we employ to avoid extremes of wealth and poverty in our society? Should we have such laws? Why or why not?
3. How could the church avoid such extremes? Should it be concerned about doing that?
4. Which right has the higher priority: the right to resources necessary to earn a living or the right to private property?
5. How should the rich resources of the U.S. be used in light of the global economic situation?
6. What percentage of your own allowance or income do you give? To whom? Why? How important is that to you?

Summary and Conclusion:

To conclude, ask students to write out individual self-contracts in which they outline some commitments they will fulfill over the next three months. Have this contract include:

*   Three steps they will take to become more informed about poverty in the U.S. and in the world;
*   Two things they will do to become more informed about legislation that affects poverty;
*   Two steps they will take to learn what the church in general is doing about poverty;

- The outline of a specific plan to learn about what their church is doing and what they can do individually and as a church about dealing with poverty.

Possible activities could include:
1. reading books and magazines
2. investigating and supporting relief organizations
3. evaluating personal giving and making a financial commitment
4. joining an organization that directly aids the poor
5. joining a group that lobbies in behalf of the poor
6. (have the group brainstorm other ideas)

After students have listed various activities, have them jot a date next to each activity as their commitment to have it completed by that time.

Note: With an ongoing class, this could become a group project, with small committees of two to three assigned various research tasks and a target date to report back to the larger group. At the end of three months, students should evaluate their goals and write new ones.

Suitcase Survival

by Jane Felthauser

Age: Adult

Setting: Group

Time: About 60 minutes

Goal: To offer participants an opportunity to personally identify with needs of the poor and to experience how the values they presently espouse would weather a challenge

Leader Preparation: Paper and pencils for all participants and a Bible with concordance; the list of questions written out on poster paper so all participants can see them; be prepared to lead a concluding group discussion

Scripture: Proverbs 3:25–28; 14:20; 22:2 Matthew 6:25–34; Romans 8:35–39; 2 Corinthians 8:9; Hebrews 13:1–3, 5–6; James 5:1–6; 1 John 3:16–18

The Exercise:
  A. Ask participants to list 10 items they would pack in a suitcase if those items were to become the only things they owned, and they would need them in order to survive. Included in the 10 items must be all of their clothing. During this part of the exercise, no talking is allowed.
  B. Then explain the rest of the assignment: Suddenly your group (each with suitcase) finds itself transported to the outskirts of a large, unfamiliar city. Your assignment is to survive for three months. For most of fifteen of the days, it rains and is rather chilly. No one gives you anything free of charge, except for one free dinner sponsored by a charity group one night.
  C. Turn the group loose to grapple with their assignment, and put up the following questions where everyone can see them.

1. How do you feel at first, facing this challenge?
2. What do you personally need in order to survive?
3. What do you have that someone else needs? Do you need it?
4. What does someone else have that you need? Do they need it?
5. Is it possible to share the things that both you and the other person need?
6. Could you meet anyone's needs by pooling resources?
7. Is there anything you could sell?
8. Is there anything else you could do to get money?
9. What would you do with the money? On whom would you spend it?
10. How would you eat?
11. Would you work together or independently?
12. Would you sacrifice any needs or comforts for someone else?
13. Would you sacrifice yourself or someone else if not all could survive?
14. Would you sacrifice for a particular person(s), but not for others? Why?

D. Lead a group discussion using the following questions:
1. How do you feel now?
2. Do you think this is a situation that many people actually face?
3. List some groups that may have had a survival experience like this. *Leader:* Remember Vietnamese boat people, illegal aliens, the mentally ill, escaped prisoners in Europe during WWII, war in Rwanda, famine in Ethiopia, or a number of U.S. citizens during the Great Depression.
4. How does that affect you?

Summary and Conclusion:
Conclude with the following questions:
1. How would this situation affect your trust in God?
2. How would your trust in God affect your response to this situation?

Have group members take turns reading the Scripture passages to each other.

That's Where My Money Goes

by Jane Felthauser

Age: Adult

Setting: Group

Time: About 60 minutes

Goal: To give participants an opportunity to examine their beliefs and attitudes about the poor and to compare them with scriptural values

Leader Preparation: The list of characters ready, with signs for each actor to wear for easy identification; be ready to lead the discussion; a Bible with a concordance

Scripture: Proverbs 14:20; 22:2; 2 Corinthians 8:9; James 5:1–6; 1 John 3:16–18

The Exercise:
Resource Allocation Role Play
 A. Each student will play the role of one of the following characters. (If there are more students, create more characters.)

wealthy business man ("redneck") ($)   mother on welfare
conservative politician (B)   liberal politician (B)
middle-class housewife   famine victim in Africa (n.v.)
wealthy and influential doctor ($)   migrant farm worker
illegal alien factory worker (n.v.)   small-town pastor

 B. *The Situation:* $250,000 is available for allocation to any of the following causes (in any percentages):

1. Famine relief (worldwide)
2. Public school funding
3. Development of agribusiness
4. Environmental controls
5. Local feeding program for children of parents on welfare
6. Regulation and improvement of factory conditions
7. Construction of an international park near the capitol
8. Funding for the American Medical Association

C. The Rules:

> The teacher will act as moderator while the actors discuss what percentage of the money should go to what cause. Each actor has one vote in the decision-making process except those marked *n.v.* *All* actors have a voice in expressing their concerns. Actors indicated by *$* may offer bribes to actors indicated by *B*. Actors indicated by *$* or *B* may have twice as many opportunities to speak as the other actors.
>
> After discussion and presentation of their concerns by each of the actors, actors must vote on which causes rightly deserve the most funding. Then, following up to ten more minutes of discussion, they must vote on which cause will receive the highest amount of funding, second highest, etc., and if possible, will designate which percent of the money will go for each.

Summary and Conclusion:

Conclude by discussing the following questions:
1. How did you feel?
2. What factors influenced the decisions you made?
3. How well do you think the role you played represents the opinion of the U.S. population in general?
4. Do you think the final decision was fair?
5. How do you think the decision should have been different? Why?
6. With which role were you personally most sympathetic? Why?
7. What new insights did you gain into public responsibilities, personal needs, and the process of policy making?
8. How would the decision the group made affect each individual involved?
9. Does God have an opinion? (See Scriptures listed and delve for others.)
10. How might we bring God's opinion into practical application?

A Friend in Need

by Gordon West

Age: Adult

Setting: Any number—a good discipleship exercise

Time: 25 minutes

Goal: To allow participants to identify as a value that people are more important than things, to identify ways in which their behavior does not line up with this value, and to devise a plan to bring their behavior more into line with their professed value

Leader Preparation: Paper and pens for each participant

Scripture: 1 John 3:16–18

The Exercise:
1. Pass out paper and pens to all participants.
2. Ask participants to think about the neediest person they know. Preferably, this should be an individual they know personally who has material needs. If they don't know any individuals with needs, they may choose a people group or an organization. Allow three to five minutes for this part.
3. Have each person write down the name of the needy individual.
4. Divide into pairs. (Married people should not pair up with their spouses for this exercise.) Designate person A and person B in the pair. Have As tell Bs ten good reasons why they have not done anything for the needy person on the paper. Then, reverse roles. Allow about ten minutes for this step. (This exercise assumes, probably accurately, that the participants are not actively helping the needy around them.)
5. Now, have As tell Bs five good reasons why they should and could help the needy person. Then, let Bs tell As. Allow five minutes.

Summary and Conclusion:

With the group as a whole invite participants to share how they felt about this exercise. Make sure the tensions that exist around giving up wealth, time, and convenience are addressed. Contrast that effort with the value of a human being. Allow five minutes or use as much more time as is available for this final discussion. Conclude by reading the Scripture to the group—unless a participant has already read it to everyone.

Exercise Ten

· ·

All's Fair in Love and War

by Alan Knott

Age: Adult

Setting: Group

Time: About 90 minutes

Goal: To stimulate participants to clarify and identify scriptural answers to moral dilemmas in Corrie Ten Boom's life. This exercise will create a cognitive dissonance in order to open up new ways of thinking about moral judgments beyond the "law and order" approach of stage 4 in Kohlberg's stages (see appendix 1). Corrie Ten Boom's life is also a role model for a godly perspective in grappling with moral dilemmas.

Leader Preparation: Obtain the film *The Hiding Place,* about Corrie Ten Boom's life, and necessary equipment to show it (If all else fails, key sections of her life story could be read aloud to the class, but this would be a poor

· ·

second choice); Handouts of discussion questions and a Bible for each participant, a board to write on for group discussion, and a concordance

Scripture: Matthew 22:36–40

The Exercise:
A. Show the movie to the group. To make this as much fun as possible, offer popcorn and soda pop and schedule this project as a special evening. Before the movie starts, ask participants to observe for the following facts: Did Corrie break the law? How many of the Ten Commandments did she break?
B. After the movie is over, divide the crowd into small groups of about five each and have them discuss the following items:
 1. When Corrie hid the Jews in her house, did she break the law? In the process of saving the Jews, did she break any of the Ten Commandments? List all the ones she broke.
 2. How could a Christian possibly be willing to break the Ten Commandments—isn't that wrong? How do you think Corrie settled this in her own mind?
 3. Are there any higher laws we can think of that might help us evaluate this situation?
 4. What would you do if you were in Corrie's shoes?
 5. What feelings would you struggle with while making your decision?
 6. Was it just for Corrie to be sent to the concentration camp? Why or why not?
 7. Are there any principles in the Bible that might help us understand or evaluate these kinds of difficult moral choices? (Read Matthew 22:36–40.)

Summary and Conclusion:
Reassemble the large group for a discussion of what the small groups concluded. Focus on Jesus' statement that the principles of love for God and love for one's neighbor supersede all other moral laws.

. . . .

To Obey or Not to Obey

by Wayne Blanchard

Age: Adult (or older youth)

Setting: Discipleship groups or Sunday school classes

Time: 45 minutes

Goal: To let participants experience the feelings involved in an obedience/authority conflict and to make them sensitive to the difficulties experienced by those who have authority over them

Leader Preparation: Bibles, pencils and paper, and at least one concordance for reference

Scripture: Acts 4:13–20; 9:1–22; Romans 13:1–7; Hebrews 13:17

The Exercise:
1. Have participants read Acts 9:1–22. (Perhaps one person could be assigned to read it aloud in a modern version while the others follow along.)
2. Hand out paper and pencils, and ask participants to imagine that they are Ananias. Have them write an account of all that happened in these verses, using the first person. Ask them to add what their feelings would have been and the thoughts going through their minds as the story unfolds.
3. Next, each participant should list some personal applications about what this chapter teaches him or her about obedience.
4. Divide the class into groups of two. From these groups have one member volunteer to be the authority figure and the other to be the

. . . .

employee. Have the groups role-play the following: The employee works for a large manufacturing firm as an accountant. One day the supervisor asks the accountant to cover up some illegal transactions he or she has made. Then, have the pairs reverse roles.

Summary and Conclusion:
After the role play, resume the large group discussion.
1. How did you feel when playing the role of the employee and you were asked to do this? Did you feel as if you had to comply because of the supervisor's authority? Why or why not?
2. How did you feel when playing the role of the supervisor and your employee would or would not obey?
3. Have you ever found yourself in a similar situation? How did you handle it?
4. Is it ever right to disobey someone in authority? Give Scriptures to back up your answer.
5. How do you make the decision when to obey and when to disobey?

Exercise Twelve

The World's Mold

by Betty Jamison

Age: Adult; with slight adjustments, this exercise would work well for Junior High and High School

Setting: Groups of 5–30 people for either leadership or discipleship planning retreats, board meetings, training sessions, small study groups, or Sunday school classes

Time: 45–60 minutes

Goal: For participants to become more aware of the world's value system in order to recognize it, combat it, and notice how it influences them

Leader Preparation: A blackboard and an overhead with blank transparencies and markers or a large blank flip chart; Bibles and at least one concordance

Scripture: Matthew 6:3; Romans 12:1–2; Ephesians 4:1–16; Colossians 3:1–10; 2 Timothy 3:16–17; Titus

The Exercise:
  A. Begin with a discussion of Romans 12:1–2.
    1. What items are contrasted in verse 2?
    2. The Phillip's translation reads, "Don't let the world around you squeeze you into its own mold." What are some ways that the world tries to mold people? (Examples: advertising, peer pressure, movies)
    3. Let's brainstorm for a minute (using blackboard or flip chart). What are some of the values the world says we should have?
    4. Look over this list and determine the top three values.
    5. In contrast, let's make a list of some of the values the Bible says we should have. List these on the chart and vote to determine the top three.
    6. How can we as Christians cultivate biblical values and combat the worldly values? (Divide a large group into small groups of three to five people and have each group look at a different Scripture passage. Have the smaller groups report back to the large group.
  B. Leader plays devil's advocate.
    1. One of the ways we can cultivate biblical values is to dialogue with each other about why those values are important, thereby thinking through why we believe in them.
    2. Pretend I am a non-Christian coworker who wants to know why you hold these top 3 biblical values. Let's take turns explaining why each of us holds one of the three values. Who will be first? Allow 15 to 20 minutes for this part.
    3. Try to make sure each person has a chance to defend a value. If necessary, break up into smaller groups and have members take turns at the non-Christian role.

Summary and Conclusion:
  Review the top worldly and biblical values. Explain why we have chosen to live by the biblical ones and how those can combat the worldly values.

The Apartment Choice

by Mark Stanson

Age: Adult

Setting: Groups, including women's groups and golden-agers

Time: 60 minutes

Goal: To give participants an opportunity to prize and cherish their values in the face of a moral dilemma

Leader Preparation: Be prepared to read the story to the group (or arrange for someone to dramatize it for the group); Bible, concordances, and a blackboard or something to write on

Scripture: Up to the class to find and share (try Luke 1:37)

The Exercise:
Let's pretend that your name is Milly, age seventy. You live in the same shabby apartment complex as your friend Harold, seventy-five. Both of you are retired. Harold worked hard for twenty-five years to put away a nest egg for his old age, and he has a small pension from the company as well. Still it's hard to meet even basic living expenses the way inflation is driving up prices. As a widow you barely survive from month to month on Social Security benefits. You both have grown children, but none with extra space to take in a parent. Besides, you prefer independence. You are a devout Christian, supervise the church nursery, and have been a dedicated churchgoer all your life.

You and Harold have become friends because you share a number of interests and help each other endure the pressures and loneliness of life. You get together from time to time to share a dinner in your little apartment, run errands, or attend social events at church.

Then, you both receive notice from the owner that rent on your apartments will go up 20 percent, effective immediately. Looking over the alternatives, you know you will have to move to an even cheaper apartment in a more dangerous neighborhood. Harold feels bad about this, but he feels even worse about losing your friendship. You know you will miss him a lot, too. Close to tears you say, "Maybe I'll just move into a retirement home. I've read that there are places that will take care of you if you sign over your Social Security checks to them."

"Those places are awful," says Harold. "You'd hate it."

"I know," you say, "but I don't see any other choice."

Harold becomes indignant. "Let's fight!"

"I'd love to fight it, but I don't know how."

"I know!" Harold says, "You can move in with me! We'll cut rent and utilities in half that way, and even save money on food!"

You're shocked. "Oh, Harold!"

"Why not? It's a nice clean place."

"Getting married at our age?" You look down at your shoes.

"Oh, we wouldn't get married. Couldn't. We'd lose some Social Security if they found out, and we'd be no better off than we are right now."

You are silent. How could you live with a man without marrying him? This goes against your deepest moral convictions. What would your children say? Your friends? Your church? And wouldn't you be cheating on your Social Security? You're not sure about that part, but this whole arrangement would violate everything you've always believed.

Summary and Conclusion:
  A. After presenting Milly's story, present the following five options. Ask each participant to choose one of them.
      1. It's very important not to be a burden on your children or society. Harold is a decent person, and you are desperate for a safe place to live. You take a deep breath and tell Harold you'll live with him.
      2. Everything in you tells you this is wrong. How could you possibly use the money from your husband's Social Security earnings to live with another man? But you feel torn. Reluctantly you say *no* to Harold and hope he'll come see you in the retirement home after you move.
      3. Even though it's hard to accept, you realize your basic need is for a decent home that you can afford and good companionship. You decide Harold's arrangement is practical and will benefit both of you.
      4. You're torn by your alternatives. You want the approval of your friends, your children, and your church, but where are they now? You decide the mutual affection between you and Harold has priority, so you'll move into his apartment.
      5. Marriage and family are the bedrock of your life. Living with Harold would betray the customs, morals, and rules you've stood for all

your life. You opt for the retirement home.
B. Now, share your choices as a group and talk about why you chose as you did.
C. Next, brainstorm options that were not on the list, if any.
D. Finally, apply Scripture to each option. Challenge the class to locate promises from God that Milly can claim at this time.

Exercise Fourteen

· ·

Boarding School Blues

by Tim A. Davis

Age: Youth, Adult, or Families (especially useful as part of a missions emphasis)

Setting: A group that acts out an improvised drama

Time: About 60 minutes

Goal: For participants to evaluate moral choices that influence responsibilities to ministry and family

Leader Preparation: Bibles for all, several concordances; a blackboard will be helpful; make sure in advance you will have group members willing to be actors

Scripture: Luke 14:26–27; Romans 8:28, 34–39; 1 Corinthians 7:32–33, 35; Ephesians 6:1; Colossians 3:2; 1 Timothy 5:8; 1 Peter 3:8–17, and others the class will look up as part of the discussion

The Exercise:
A. The purpose of the drama is to bring out the moral conflicts that can

· ·

occur when different members of the family disagree about family and ministry priorities and to prepare the group to discuss these issues. There are 5 roles, and each person should follow his or her own intuition in playing out the role, inventing dialogue and actions as the drama unfolds, within the limits of the character sketch for each part. This sort of exercise is usually more effective if the participants choose to slightly overemphasize their points rather than play them down.

B. *[The scene: A missionary family lives with a tribe in a remote village in Sri Lanka, isolated from typical American life, where the parents are studying the language in order to translate the Bible for the tribe. The village lacks, in addition to other comforts, an appropriate school, so the parents teach their children at home in the early grades. By the fourth grade, the parents must send their children away to an international school. Then, the children only see their parents once a month for a few days. The parents have been taught that God will make up to their children anything they have to give up for the parents' ministry.]*

C. Cast of characters
   1. **Andrew,** the father, grew up on a ranch, doesn't mind roughing it, loves the challenge of linguistics, and spends hours hanging out with the tribe or with his battery-operated computer analyzing the structure of this tribal language. It's clear to him that this is where God wants him—if only his family could understand that and be more cooperative!
   2. **Beth,** the mother, grew up in a strict, legalistic home and feels upset any time things aren't perfect—and they certainly aren't now. She is utterly torn between her need to be the perfect, loyal wife and support her husband's work and her need to be the perfect mother to their three children who can't see the sense in what Dad does for a living. She knows that God calls His people to be faithful unto death and to be willing to suffer for the sake of righteousness.
   3. **Paul,** fifteen, has experienced quite enough "suffering for the Lord," in his own opinion. When he was just seven years old, he agreed to come to Sri Lanka. But now, he feels resentful and unloved—especially because of the separation from his family that attending school causes. If Dad really loved God at all, he would care for his own family first. Doesn't he realize that he's destroying the entire family?
   4. **Amy,** eleven, is quiet and shy. After two years in Sri Lanka, she has been unable to make friends at school. Many nights she cries herself to sleep, but she would never want her parents to know because she adores her father and is loyal to her family. If she were honest, though, she would admit that she hates this school arrangement.
   5. **Chip,** seven, is doing second-grade work and is still at home. He

senses the tensions and misses his older brother and sister but doesn't really understand the issues. Once, he asked his mom, "Will you make me go away, too?"

D. As the drama opens, the entire family is sitting around the table finishing a meal when the issue comes up. The conversation is tense as Paul asks, "Why can't we just live together like normal people?" Andrew, the father, responds, "But God has called me to this work."

E. Before starting the drama, challenge the entire group to think of as many Scriptures as possible that would relate to the situation about to be portrayed. Read all of the above drama notes to the entire group, and then set the stage with five chairs and a volunteer for each role. Let the drama unfold as the volunteers interact, and if necessary, suggest possible dialogue to the participants to keep the action lively. Finish the role play after each character has had ample opportunity to make his or her position known, but without coming to any definite conclusions.

(No matter how many different groups you use this exercise with, you will find that the drama plays out differently each time.)

Summary and Conclusion:

Conclude with a group discussion focusing on how to apply God's Word to the family's dilemma. Encourage people to use the concordances to look up the verses. If the group is slow to come up with verses, have a few ready yourself.

Encourage the group to empathize with each family member and try to make a scriptural defense for each position. List positive and negative aspects of each position. Use the board to record the group's input.

Ask the participants to determine what they would do in this situation, and why, backing up their decision with Scripture.

Note: This exercise could stimulate the group to more inspired and steadfast prayer for missionaries. The leader could have a list of missionaries the church supports ready to send home with the class, and could obtain a promise from class members to pray for them during the upcoming week.

Exercise Fifteen

. . . .

Conflict Resolution

by Gwen McKay

Age: Adult

Setting: Groups of 10–15; could be used at a leadership retreat, training session, discipleship group, or two one-hour Sunday school classes

Time: 2 hours

Goal: To help each adult begin to internalize working through conflict in a healthy manner (Healthy resolution of conflict is an essential goal or value in any setting especially in the church)

Leader Preparation: Go through the exercise yourself, so that you become familiar with the questionnaire and the interpretation of the scores; Copies of the Questionnaire (pp. 209–11) and pencils available for each participant, a blackboard, overhead, etc, to present the facts about styles of conflict; Bibles and at least one concordance will make it easy for participants to contribute Scripture quotes to the discussion

Scripture: Matthew 5:23–25; 18:15–17; Luke 17:3–2; Romans 14:19; Galatians 2:11–16

The Exercise:
   A. Answer the Questionnaire
        Have participants fill out the Questionnaire, indicating their answers by circling one of the numbers between 1 and 5. One represents "You've got to be kidding! This never happens with me." Five represents "This always happens with me."
        Encourage participants to go with their first instinct and not to go back and change answers.

. . . .

Questionnaire

Directions: Circle the correct number (1= "never me," 5= "always me")

1. I am often confused about what I want to be, how I want to act, and what I want to do.
    1   2   3   4   5

2. I often go into meetings without having written down any clear-cut goals.
    1   2   3   4   5

3. I often feel I am having a battle within myself.
    1   2   3   4   5

4. I am often unsure what I want to happen in the confrontation.
    1   2   3   4   5

5. Others often tell me they can't figure out what it is that I want.
    1   2   3   4   5

6. In the midst of an argument, I sometimes like the confrontation, because at least someone is paying attention to me.
    1   2   3   4   5

7. I frequently find myself fighting a policy simply because I don't like the person presenting it.
    1   2   3   4   5

8. When I am in a conflict with someone, I feel better if I have more power than he or she does.
    1   2   3   4   5

9. I prefer job descriptions in which my duties are not clearly defined.
    1   2   3   4   5

10. I do not like to have people working under me. I would rather do all the tasks myself.
    1   2   3   4   5

11. I tend to be more concerned that I achieve my goals than how the other person feels.
    1   2   3   4   5

12. I make out a list of things I need to do each day, and nothing gets in my way of getting the items accomplished.
   1   2   3   4   5

13. I love the feeling of winning at all costs.
   1   2   3   4   5

14. When I am addressing problems with others, I am more concerned that my relationship with them remains healthy than that I achieve my goals.
   1   2   3   4   5

15. I will often give up my personal goals for a good friend.
   1   2   3   4   5

16. I work at staying out of conflicts with my friends because I don't want the relationship to be damaged.
   1   2   3   4   5

17. I often find that conflicts end up with my losing both the relationship and my goals.
   1   2   3   4   5

18. The best way to deal with conflict is to withdraw entirely, and someday it will all be forgotten.
   1   2   3   4   5

19. I believe that any relationship with conflict in it is an unhealthy one.
   1   2   3   4   5

20. I believe that I can never get everything I want through conflict. Instead I need to give a little to get a little.
   1   2   3   4   5

21. I usually feel OK about pushing for my goals, as long as I don't jeopardize the relationship I have with others.
   1   2   3   4   5

22. I feel it's only fair in a conflict to let the other guy get some of what he wants, no matter what my desires are.
   1   2   3   4   5

23. I am very concerned that both my goals and the other person's goals are achieved. I also want the relationship between us to be enhanced as a result of the conflict.
    1   2   3   4   5

24. I believe that it is often possible for both parties to achieve their goals.
    1   2   3   4   5

   A. Discussion:
        This questionnaire deals with three possible causes of conflict.
        •   **Confusion** is reflected by a high score in questions 1–5.
        •   **Concealment** is indicated by a high score in questions 6–7.
        •   **Desire for power and control** is indicated by high scores in questions 8–10.
        In addition, there are five methods for dealing with conflict:
    1. *Win/lose:* This approach values achievement of a goal over the relationships involved. "Win at all costs even if the relationship is damaged" is the motto for this style. High scores in questions 11–13 may reflect this approach.
    2. *Accommodation:* Concern for the relationship and a willingness to give up personal goals for the sake of the relationship characterize this style. Concern over loosing a relationship dominates this approach. Questions 14–16 probe this issue.
    3. *Avoidance:* Hopelessness over the conflict colors this approach because this person sees that the goals and the relationships may both be lost as a result of conflict. This person expends a lot of effort to avoid conflict, and if caught in one, will withdraw. High scores in questions 17–19 might point to this style.
    4. *Compromise:* This approach to conflict believes that everybody has to give up something in order to meet in the middle. "I'll give up some of my goals if you will, too." By allowing the other party in the conflict to get at least some of what he or she wants, this individual hopes to preserve the relationship after the conflict is over. Questions 20–22 deal with this style.
    5. *Win/win:* This style places a high value on both the goals of the participants and on the quality of their relationship. This individual desires that both people in a conflict achieve their goals, as well as wanting the relationship to be enhanced as a result. This person actively works toward that end. High score in questions 23–24 might reflect this orientation.
        Though each of the above styles is appropriate under certain circumstances, research has shown that regular use of some styles is more likely to promote healthy and constructive use of conflict than other styles. To apply this research practically, one would first

try the win/win approach. If that fails, then the next method to use, in order, would be compromise, accommodation, win/lose, and finally avoidance.*

B. Role play: After participants have received the above information, divide the participants into groups of two or three. Assign each group one of the five conflict management styles and have each develop a 1 or 2 minute skit illustrating the style. Have each group present its skit before the whole group.

Summary and Conclusion:
Lead the group in a discussion with the following questions as a guideline:

1. Which type of conflict management do you identify with?
2. What do you see as the benefits and drawbacks of each style? (Use a blackboard to list these as the group identifies them.)
3. With whom are we most likely to encounter conflict? (family, employees, friends, church members)
4. Can you think of any individuals in Scripture who dealt with conflict? Which different methods do they use? How did their situations work out? (see Scriptures listed)
5. Do you feel you have the ability to see yourself as you really are?
6. How have others perceived your management of conflict in the past?
7. With the Lord's guidance and help, what situations might you be involved in this week where you could demonstrate a healthier conflict management style? Would you be willing to select one situation and pray about it specifically?

---

* This information is taken from G. Douglas Lewis, *Resolving Church Conflict: A Case Study Approach for Local Congregations* (San Francisco: Harper and Row, 1981), 78–79.

Creative Representations

Age: Adult and Youth

Setting: Groups of 6 to about 16 (especially helpful as an icebreaker with people forming into a new group)

Time: 10 minutes for the creative project(s), 5 minutes per person to talk about the creation, and 5–10 minutes to summarize

Goal: To lay the groundwork for people to care for one another by getting to know each other better; participants will be asked to think about who they are and given an opportunity to talk about their findings with others

Leader Preparation: Decide which tools you want to use—wire, long pipecleaners, clay, or Play-Doh®—enough for each participant

Scripture: 1 Corinthians 12:12–20; Philippians 2:3–4

The Exercise:
Give each person a piece of wire about a foot long. Ask each person to create an object with that piece of wire that depicts his or her spiritual pilgrimage. When all have finished, have them explain why they shaped the object the way they did. This will give them a chance to talk about their struggles and successes. It is amazing how quiet people open up.

Other applications:
1. A design to illustrate how they want other people to remember them.
2. One to illustrate their conversion experience.
3. One to illustrate their greatest spiritual victory.

Summary and Conclusion:
Read the Scripture, and point out any common themes that may emerge in the art work or in the things people share.

Exercise Seventeen

Election Campaign

by Jeanne Williams

Age: High School through Adult

Setting: Group of 9–24 individuals (3 groups of 3–8 each)

Time: About 40 minutes

Goal: To show that virtues cannot make up for sins; participants will be probing the alternatives to the Scriptures listed below, and are therefore at the step of choosing from alternatives (see pp. 8–9)

Leader Preparation: Biographical sketch for each of the three candidates; pens and paper for each group member, at least one Bible for reference

Scripture: James 2:10; 1 John 1:8–10

The Exercise:
A. Divide the class into three groups.
B. Assign one candidate to each group, and give the group its candidate's "biography":
   1. M. T. Hart, the first candidate, is known for his total honesty. He never lies. He is also very loving, yet he is not a believer.
   2. The second candidate, I. M. Sly, is the most loving person you have ever met. She loves everybody! She is also a believer, but she often lies.
   3. The third candidate, Willie Share, is an honest man, and also a believer. However, he loves nobody but himself.
C. Each group must write a three to five minute campaign speech telling why its candidate is the best. They should lean heavily on the candidate's virtues and try to show why this person's weakness is not so bad in light of all the good. Allow ten minutes to prepare these speeches.
D. Have one member of each group deliver the speech.

Summary and Conclusion:
1. Was anyone convinced that your candidate was best for the job? Why or why not?
2. Are there ever virtues or positive traits so admirable that it overshadows the sin in your life?
3. Is there ever a sin that is unimportant? If yes, which one(s)?
4. Read James 2:18 aloud to the group and ask what it means.
5. James has just been talking about showing partiality to the rich, which was a common and accepted thing to do in Bible times. What are some sins we overlook today because they are socially acceptable?

Read 1 John 1:8–10, and allow time for participants to give God permission to reveal sin and to cleanse whatever He reveals.

Exercise Eighteen

The Golden Rule and Divorce

Age: Adult

Setting: Discipleship or leadership groups, Sunday school class, small group, or training session

Time: About 60 minutes

Goal: To stimulate participants to consider their responsibility to Matthew 7:12 (Luke 6:21–31) in the light of contemporary justice and societal norms

Leader Preparation: A blackboard, Bibles, and concordances for reference

Scripture: Matthew 7:12; Luke 6:21–31; 1 Peter 3:9–11

The Exercise:

1. Write on the blackboard: Agree or disagree?
   It's all right for a Christian to take another Christian to court to settle a dispute.

2. After the group is seated, relate the following situation:

   Wayne and Ann have been married for twelve years and have two children in grade school. Over the last few years they seem to have grown more distant and quarrelsome with each other. They attended a Marriage Encounter weekend a year ago, but it had no lasting effect. Suddenly Ann is served divorce papers by Wayne's attorney. Ann talks Wayne into seeing their pastor, who recommends that they pursue counseling before they do anything rash. Wayne is adamant that he has struggled long enough and wants out.

   During the ensuing week, Ann's best friend (who has suffered divorce herself) visits her to console her and offer some advice. She reminds Ann that she will need an attorney since she has no marketable skills and will need the legal certainty of adequate provision for herself and her family. This sounds too aggressive to

Building Biblical Values

Ann, who has witnessed some divorce battles from a distance. Later, her prayer group counsels her that legal action on her part would only aggravate the situation and eliminate any chance of Wayne's changing his mind. What should Ann do?

3. Have the class brainstorm any possible options for Ann; write them on the board
4. Read the Scripture passage. Divide into groups of four and narrow the list on the board to those possibilities not eliminated by this passage. Let each group include other Scriptures that influence their decision as well.
5. Have each group summarize their results, and alter the brainstorming list on the board accordingly.

Summary and Conclusion:
1. Itemize the scriptural principles that apply. Do they conflict with or complement Matthew 7:12?
2. Get back into small groups and have them choose the two most important principles. Write a statement to Ann, as her friend, answering her question, "What should I do?"
3. As a class, discuss the possible consequences of each bit of advice. See if the class as a whole can agree on one of the suggestions as the most practical counsel based on scriptural values.

Exercise Nineteen

· ·

Graph Your Spiritual Pilgrimage

Age: Adult and Youth

Setting: Group

Time: 60 minutes

· ·

Goal: Using a graph to measure past spiritual progress, participants will be able to see and come to value God's presence in their personal history as meaningful and useful to their development. This should encourage them toward further spiritual growth.

Leader Preparation: Graph paper for each person; a blackboard and some Bibles also helpful

Scripture: 1 Peter 2:2; 2 Peter 1:3–11

The Exercise:
  A. The graph
    1. After all have a piece of graph paper, instruct them to place the paper in front of them the long way and draw a line from left to right across the middle of the paper. This line represents "average." The top of the paper represents "absolutely fabulous" and the bottom is "the pits."
    2. Next, instruct each person to draw a line down the middle of the paper from top to bottom, dividing it in half, and then 2 more lines, one on each side, parallel to that one so that the paper ends up being divided up into fourths vertically. Tell participants to divide their ages by four, and assign a quarter of their lives to each quadrant. (A sixteen-year-old will have four years in each quadrant. A forty-year-old will have ten years in each quadrant.)
    3. Now tell them: You are going to make a graph to represent your spiritual progress. Starting at the far left is your birth. We were all born without Christ. Make a little cross at the point where you received Christ. Some folks may have had a "spiritual awakening" before receiving Jesus, and others may have been "in the pits." Let your graph reflect your spiritual condition as you perceived it, before, during, and immediately after your conversion.
    4. Next, think over the years since your conversion and the progress you have made. Remind yourself of the high points and low points and mark them on your graph. When you get to the far right, it should represent where you are today.
    5. Feel free to label some of these spots (for example, going to Bible camp, getting married, missionary work-trip to Mexico, or joining a prayer group). Other items you could include: most difficult trial, times when God intervened, most exciting adventure with God, a time I really missed the mark, or a time of great illumination from God.
    6. Mark the various events that seemed to either hinder or stimulate spiritual growth for you.

B. After charts are done
   1. Leader, encourage people to analyze their graphs. What criteria have they used to define their growth?
   2. Experience shows that most graphs will reflect people's emotional feelings about their Christian lives. If that is the case, have them draw a second line showing how they think God has perceived their growth.
   3. Discuss what guidelines they think God would use. (Many people don't have a very clear or objective view of how God does perceive growth.) Use 1 Peter 2:2 as a springboard for discussion.
   4. Also, here are some factors to consider when evaluating growth. If a board is available, list them there:
      a) Dependence on God—your faith
      b) Prayer life—time spent, sincerity, and earnestness
      c) Fruits of the Spirit—do they show?
      d) Active in telling others about Jesus
      e) Understanding/grasp of Scripture and Christian ethics or lifestyle
      f) Level of concern for others
      g) How you deal with temptations
      h) Proportion of time, money, and energy given in service
      i) Response to trials, pain, and disappointments
      j) Amount of time you spend in worship and Bible study
      k) Ways you've allowed God to change your values

Summary and Conclusion:
   1. Now that we know where we are today and how we got there, turn your paper over and mark where you want to be, with God's help, in one year and in five years.
   2. What do you think will need to happen in order to grow in this way?
Conclude by reading 2 Peter 1:3–11, to see what God has supplied to stimulate and support our spiritual development.

Note: This exercise can be adapted to assist with team-building by adding a step between one and two where participants share their charts with each other. In a small group, everyone can share in turn. In a large group, have them subdivide into minigroups of three. Doing this step will add between fifteen to thirty minutes to the total time of the exercise.

Love and Accountability

by Penny Thome

Age: Adult

Setting: 10–30 persons, especially church leadership and discipleship groups

Time: 4 one-hour sessions

Goal: To provide an opportunity to apply personal ideals and scriptural principles to a realistic situation.

Leader Preparation: Thoroughly study the scenario, questions, and Scriptures to have a clear understanding of the issues raised. Think about additional questions or Scriptures that you might want to bring up for discussion. This material was originally presented in a small Sunday school class over four weeks. In another setting, 2 two-hour sessions might work, but time in between sessions to think is important to the process. Each participant will need a copy of the scenario, sheet of discussion questions, and a Bible. A concordance should be available for reference.

Scripture: Scripture listings integrated throughout the study

The Exercise:
Introduction
Please read over the following scenario in its entirety. Then read over the attached list of questions and Scriptures. Use a concordance to locate any additional Scriptures that you think would also be relevant. Decide what counsel you would give to the group in the scenario. What actions do they need to take? What attitudes do they need to hold in order to obey Scriptures?

Week 1

A small group of families (all born-again Christians) has known each other for over twenty-five years. Through the years, they have helped one another in practical matters, gone to retreats, shared Bible studies, prayer times, and fun times.

There always seemed to be some tension in one couple. Walter and Mary would erupt with sarcastic remarks at unexpected moments. Some couples in the group requested prayer and counsel at times for marital tension. Walt and Mary made it quite clear that they regarded anything beyond superficial concern intrusive, so the group did not probe.

Week 1 questions for discussion:*

1. Have you ever been in a situation where you sensed tension just beneath the surface? How did it affect you?
2. If 1 member of the body has a problem, does it affect the well-being of the body as a whole? (see Deuteronomy 13:5; Romans 12:4–5; 1 Corinthians 12:12, 26; 2 Corinthians 2:5; Ephesians 4:25, 5:29–30)
3. What responsibility does the group have to address the discomfort manifested by Walt and Mary? (see Romans 15:14; 1 Peter 3:8–12; 1 John 5:16)
4. If the group were to address that issue, how should they do it? (see Romans 12:6a; 15:1–3; Galatians 6:1,10; 1 Thessalonians 5:22–23)

* Be sure to back up your answers with Scriptures.

Week 2

The day eventually came when Mary and Walt announced to the group that Mary was moving out. Walt had one version of the story—Mary was abandoning the family and her duties as a wife. Mary's version was that Walt and the children ganged up on her and kicked her out.

The group invested a great deal of prayer, time, and energy in trying to assist this family. But it seemed impossible to arrive at any definition of truth or the basic facts. Their reports were widely divergent. Mary claimed that Walt was overbearing to the point of destroying her mental health. Walt, on the other hand, implied that Mary was involved with someone outside the marriage.

Both Walt and Mary sought to vindicate themselves in the group's eyes. Mary projected an attitude of open-mindedness. She acknowledged Walt's "cruelty" had forced her to extramarital interests but denied any physical involvement. She said that she wanted a reconciliation but only under conditions she would consider more humane. Walt expected the group to punish Mary. He seemed more focused on vengeance than reconciliation.

Week 2 questions for discussion:

1. If you were in this group, how would you feel about these events? Would you be tempted to take sides? Would it be important for you to establish

who is right and who is wrong? Would it be more important to have the marriage healed or the individuals healed? (see Romans 15:5–6,13)

2. If you were a group member and your own marriage had been going through difficult times, how would this affect your response?

3. What responsibilities does the group have toward Walt? Mary? Be sure to back up your reply with specific Scriptures (see Matthew 5:31–32; Romans 12:16–21; 14:19)

Week 3

Finally, Mary obtained a divorce. All four children were devastated, and everyone in the family ended up in counseling, each with a different counselor. The whole situation was very complicated and painful, and the group prayed about how to respond. Within the next year, Walt alienated the group with his bitter attitude. But Mary kept contact with the group, sharing pain and confusion, making it clear she needed and desired prayer support. Eventually, she brought a man named Pete to the group and wanted them to accept him. Meanwhile, Walt and the children insisted Mary was having an affair with Pete.

One evening, the group confronted Mary and attempted to clarify her relationship with Pete. As Christians, the group took a clear stand against sex outside of marriage. What was the nature of this relationship they were being asked to endorse? Mary vaguely acknowledged with a blush that her behavior wasn't perfect, but then who is "so perfect that we had a right to cast the first stone?" she asked. The group pressed the point of having a biblical standard for sexual behavior and that they wanted to hold her accountable. She insisted that her relationship with Pete was her own business—between her and God—and the group had absolutely no right to ask about it. But then, she promised to earnestly pray about it.

The group was in a quandary. The confrontation had been very difficult and emotionally unsettling for everyone. The group was not at all satisfied with Mary's answers yet did not want to be condemning or unloving. Had they done all they could? What else could or should they do? After all, Mary claims to be a Christian, as does Pete. Maybe it just needs some more time and prayer.

Week 3 questions for discussion:
1. Is a Christian's moral behavior private or open for discussion by other Christians? Why or why not? (see Joshua 7; Romans 14:4; 1 Corinthians 5:1–2; 2 Corinthians 2:5–7; Galatians 6:1)

2. Does *my* stance as an individual make a difference?

3. Does the Bible present an absolute standard of having no sexual relationships outside of marriage? (see Acts 15:20; Romans 13:9–10; 1 Corinthians 5:11; 6:9, 12–20; 7:12; Galatians 5:18–21; Hebrews 12:16, 13:4; Revelation 21:8)

4. How do we take a firm stand against sinful behavior without committing the sin of judging? (see Deuteronomy 17:4, 19:15–21;

Proverbs 13:21; Romans 15:1–2; 1 Corinthians 6:11; Galatians 2:14, 6:1–4)

5. Does the Bible say it's always wrong for a Christian to judge? When does the Bible condemn judging? When does it urge Christians to judge? (see Matthew 7:1–2; John 7:24; Romans 1:32–2:4, 14; 1 Corinthians 6:11, 11:13, 14:29; 1 Thessalonians 5:22–23)

6. When Mary reported that her Christian counselor said that the group was overstepping its bounds by questioning her behavior, what Scriptures would guide your response? Would the group have a duty to submit to the authority of this Christian leader? (see Matthew 18:15; Romans 15:14)

Week 4

After many months one of Walt and Mary's sons, now stationed overseas with the military, wrote a letter to each group member. In it he explained his Christian mother had taught him that sex outside of marriage was evil, and he was convinced that his mother and Pete were having sex. From his perspective, this was an intolerable situation, and he was holding Pete and his mother accountable. He made it clear he expected the rest of the body of Christ to hold them accountable as well.

Week 4 questions for discussion:

1. How do we take the stand of accepting and supporting a person unconditionally (no matter what their behavior), without committing the sin of compromise and embracing evil? (see 1 Corinthians 5:6–8; 2 Corinthians 2:7)

2. Where does the concept of mercy fit in this issue? (see 1 Timothy 1:15–16; James 2:12–13)

3. Is it truly loving to cooperate with a person who flaunts the Bible's teachings on sexual morality? (see Matthew 18:1–10; Romans 15:1–2; Galatians 6:7–9; Ephesians 5:11–14; Revelation 21:7–8)

4. What do we look for if we're seeking to help restore someone? (see Matthew 18:15–18; Luke 17:3–4; 2 Corinthians 2:4–7, 7:8–12; Galatians 6:1–2)

5. How would we know if another person is repentant? What does the Bible say about gauging repentance? (see Job 42:1–6; Psalms 51:10–12; Isaiah 30:15; Matthew 3:8; Luke 19:8–10; Acts 26:20; 1 Peter 5:10)

Summary and Conclusion:

Summarize the responsibilities the group has to each person (including God) based on Scriptures in each of the stages of this situation. Was the group a failure in God's eyes because they were not able to contribute to a happier ending to this story? Why or why not?

. . . .

Exercises for Adults

Optional bonus question: The Bible talks about committing an unrepentant brother or sister to Satan for the destruction of the flesh that the soul may be saved. What does that mean? How could it be carried out today? Is it a corporate or individual responsibility? (Luke 22:31; 1 Corinthians 2:4–7, 5:1–12; 2 Corinthians 7:8–12; 1 Timothy 1:20)

Exercise Twenty-One

Love Thy Neighbor

by DeWayne Ramsey

Age: Adult

Setting: Individuals or groups for discipleship or leadership

Time: 15–20 minutes

Goal: For participants to internalize the value of loving their neighbor

Leader Preparation: A Self-Evaluation Tool (p. 225) for each participant, and questions to stimulate group discussion

Scripture: Luke 10:25–37

The Exercise:
- A. Give the participants the self-evaluation test, and allow five minutes for them to score themselves.
- B. Questions for discussion
  1. Why did you reply the way you did?
  2. Is there a pattern for your responses?

3. What runs through your mind when you experience these situations in real life?
4. What principle are you living by?
5. Is there a biblical principle that applies to these situations? What would it be? How would it apply? (Participants may come up with a variety of passages. If the discussion needs some stimulation, read the passage from Luke. Whatever principles are mentioned, be sure to read them directly from the Bible.)

Summary and Conclusion:
1. It was socially unacceptable for Samaritans to relate with Jews. What reasons and excuses come to your mind to justify minimal involvement with neighbors?
2. What steps can you take this month to begin practicing this principle as a part of your life? Which one step will you commit to take this month, with God's help?

Self-Evaluation Tool

1. Stop to help stranded motorists.
   Never   *Always*
2. Know the neighbors in my apartment complex or on my block.
   Less than two   *More than two*
3. Have a barbecue or other activity with next-door neighbor.
   Never   *Often*
4. Set aside extra money for the sole purpose of helping an indigent.
   Never   *Often*
5. Loan personal belongings (e.g., car) to someone you know.
   Never   *Often*
6. Volunteer to help with projects for those physically unable to do the work themselves.
   Never   *Often*
7. Give up something dear (like tickets to an NFL game) to take an elderly person shopping.
   Never   *Often*
8. When you see a car accident on the side of the road, your initial response is to . . .
   Stop and help   *Look on*
9. When you see lines of people outside of a soup kitchen, your initial response is . . .
   Pity   *Compassion*

. . . .

What's Your Missions IQ?

by Lori Seed

Age: Adult

Setting: Leadership or discipleship groups

Time: 30 minutes

Goal: To stimulate participants to become more committed, involved supporters of foreign missions

Leader Preparation: A copy of What's Your Missions IQ? (p. 228) for each participant, questions to stimulate group discussion

Scripture: 3 John 5–7

The Exercise:
  A. Distribute the worksheet to everyone in the group, and explain the purpose is to help them evaluate their involvement in missions (allow ten minutes).
  B. Discussion Questions:
    1. How do you rate your involvement in each of these areas?
       10 = highly involved   1 = not involved
    2. Which do you enjoy most?
    3. In which areas should you do more?
    4. In the blank spaces provided, list any further ways a person can be involved in missions.
    5. What are the results of your involvement?
    6. What are the consequences of not being involved? For you? For the missionaries?

. . . .

C. After the group has completed the first section, have them break up into groups of four or five to answer the following questions (allow 15 minutes).
1. How do you feel about your overall commitment to missions?
2. What is the most important thing you have discovered during your participation in missions?
3. What things help or hinder your involvement?
4. What other things could you do to be involved in missions the way you want to be?
5. What changes will you make this week?

Summary and Conclusion:
Conclude the exercise with an encouragement to be more involved in foreign missions by following through on changes they want to make.

What's Your Missions IQ?
(Missions Involvement Quotient)

Ways to be Involved	Rating*	Enjoyment	Do More
Prayer	☐	☐	☐
Give regular financial support	☐	☐	☐
Give one-time financial gifts	☐	☐	☐
Write letters to missionaries	☐	☐	☐
Help missionaries on furlough	☐	☐	☐
Visit mission fields	☐	☐	☐
Become a missionary	☐	☐	☐
Meet special needs of missionaries	☐	☐	☐
Other:	☐	☐	☐
Other:	☐	☐	☐

*1 = not involved ⟶ 10 = highly involved

. . . .

Exercise Twenty-Three

. . . .

Pick Your Pilot

by Don Baldrica

Age: Adult

Setting: Discipleship or Sunday school groups

Time: 30–45 minutes

Goal: To show the value of having a quiet time and to stimulate participants to commit to having one regularly

Leader Preparation: Become familiar with this material so you can present it clearly; devotional books, tracts, or Bible study books available on how to conduct a quiet time (Check with your local Christian bookstore)

Scripture: James 1:21–25

The Exercise:
Today we are going to give each of you a chance to pick your own Air Force pilot. Let's say you are medical doctors and on one of the aircraft carriers in the middle of the Pacific Ocean. There is a medical emergency that requires your immediate assistance. You will need to take an F-1 11.

The fun part is that you get to choose the pilot who will fly you to the carrier. You have a choice from four people: Bill, Joe, Sue, or Carol. So, pick one right now. Hurry up! This is an emergency!

[The class may have some questions, such as, "Are they all pilots?" But tell them that at this point they have to choose without further information. Ask for a show of hands to indicate who each class member has picked. Choose a few people to explain why they picked as they did.]

I know it is tough to pick just by their names, so I'll help you out with some more information. If you want to change your choice, you may.

. . . .

Building Biblical Values

Bill:	5' 10"	a very generous person, born in San Francisco
Joe:	6' 0"	a very quiet person, born in St. Louis
Sue:	5' 9"	a very compassionate person, born in Kansas City
Carol:	5' 8"	a very outgoing person, born in New York City

Ask if there is anyone who would like to change his or her answer and why.

I sense you may still feel the information is incomplete. But I've given you three very important facts about each person. So, what is it you really want to know in order to make your decision? [Probably the class will want to know if they are pilots and if they know how to fly the F-1 11. At this point you kindly give then the following additional information.]

Bill:	is in the Air Force and loves to fly.
Joe:	is a bush pilot in Alaska.
Sue:	is an expert in the F-1 11 and knows every part of it.
Carol:	is in the Air Force and enjoys flying.

Ask the class if this information helps and press them to make their final decision. Most likely they will not be satisfied, so you reluctantly agree to give them 1 more piece of information, though you hate to take the time. It's getting late and you need to get on that F-1 11!

Bill:	is still in training school and has flown the F-1 11 twice.
Joe:	is one of the best twin engine pilots in the business.
Sue:	is the chief mechanic for F-1 11s, but has never flown one.
Carol:	has flown F-1 11s for 5 years on aircraft carriers.

Summary and Conclusion:

Is there anyone who wants to have someone other than Carol be the pilot?

Why did we go through this little adventure? We wanted you to have the experience of needing to make a decision and sort through what information was actually important. We saw that you didn't want to pick a pilot until you could know for sure if that person was able to fly an F-1 11. Many things didn't matter—whether they are male or female, where they are from, or even if they know a lot about the airplane. Your question was whether or not they could land on a carrier, and that would only be possible if they were experienced. That's what counted in the end.

Let's take that same idea and transfer it into how to be a mature Christian. Does it matter whether you are male or female? How tall you are, or where you were born? What you do for a living? What theoretical knowledge you have about Christianity? Remember Sue? She knew all about the F-1 11, but no one wanted to fly with her.

· ·

What does it take to make a mature Christian?

1. A mature Christian needs to know who God is in a personal way. One who doesn't know Him personally can't be a mature believer. We get to know Him personally by reading His Word and praying to Him.

2. A person doesn't instantly become a mature Christian just as someone doesn't become an instant F-1 11 pilot. It takes time and discipline. A mature Christian is someone who has spent a lot of time with God on a regular basis and not simply when they felt like it. The more time spent with God, the more mature we become. A mature perspective and a well-developed faith will help to avoid some of the struggles in life and to deal more effectively with struggles that do come.

We have a variety of materials on display to help you get going on a daily quiet time. Look them over for about 10 minutes. Then, we'll have a prayer of dedication. I'll give you an opportunity to make a commitment to spend a minimum of five minutes a day alone with God. [You could have a sign-up sheet for those willing to make a commitment in writing. Emphasize that the commitment is to stick with the project even if a person occasionally fails along the way.]

The Effect of Television Viewing on Children's Values

by Carolyn Tunnell

Age: Adult

Setting: Leaders responsible for the welfare of children, MOPS Steering Committee, Pioneer Club leaders, Sunday school teachers, and VBS leaders

Time: 45–60 minutes

Goal: To raise the level of interest and concern regarding the effect of television viewing on children's values and moral development

Leader Preparation: A copy of A Survey to Focus on Television Viewing by Children (p. 233) for each participant, pencils, questions to stimulate group discussion, Bibles, and concordances for reference; you might also want to research the names of publications with family values that offer evaluations of television programs

Scripture: Psalm 101:3; Philippians 4:8

The Exercise:
1. Distribute the surveys and pencils to participants. Explain that each person should respond with his or her general reaction to each question. About half the questions have a right or wrong answer, according to research done on the subject. Even on these questions, however, the answers are definitely open for debate.
2. After the surveys are completed, divide the large group into groups of four (separate spouses). Groups should compare their answers,

looking for the three questions on which they disagree the most. For these questions, one group member should write down the reasons the group gave to justify their responses.

3. Reunite the entire group to share responses. Although half of the questions have no correct answers, research tends to support these responses:

1. T	8. T
2. F	13. T
3. F	15. T
4. F	16. T
6. T	20. F

4. Allow time for each group to bring up relevant points for each of their 3 "debatable" questions. Allow ample time for others in the large group to respond. Current understandings or attitudes of participants may be brought into question or reinforced by the discussion.

Summary and Conclusion:

If discussion lags, try these questions:
1. Does television viewing cause children to become emotionally disturbed?
2. What types of values are portrayed in the average TV program that a child is likely to watch?
3. How high is the correlation between what children see advertised and what products they ask for? (about 70 percent) Is this beneficial? For whom?
4. What potential for teaching positive values and morals is there when using commercial television?
5. What effect does television have on your family relationships?
6. Can you think of things children find out "too soon" because they watch television?
7. Is there a standard for how much television a child should watch per day? Would this standard change with the age of the child? How could such a standard be enforced?
8. How can an interested adult get additional insights and understanding in this area?

A Survey to Focus on Television Viewing by Children

1. By showing acts of violence, commercial television places value on violence as a means to achieve goals and solve problems. T F
2. Sexual behavior shown on commercial television is realistic and helps children understand what they often encounter in their own lives. T F
3. Commercial television will effect the values and moral behaviors of all children in the same way. T F
4. All children will be disturbed by violence on television. T F
5. It would be helpful if there were a greater number of moral programs on commercial television for children to view. T F
6. Television has both a positive and a negative effect on children. T F
7. Television can strengthen family relationships. T F
8. Television viewing tends to reduce social interaction among children. T F
9. Watching television programs helps to stimulate the creativity and imagination of children. T F
10. Television advertising has an enormous influence on the desires of children. T F
11. The television networks have an obligation to present only morally responsible programs for children's viewing. T F
12. The government has the ultimate responsibility to ensure that the commercial television that children watch contains moral content.   T F
13. By viewing television programs that contain violence, children's aggressive behaviors will increase. T F
14. Parental attempts to influence television's effect on children's behavior by controlling, watching, and interpreting violence will have little effect. T F
15. Children's respect for women has been reduced by the character types in which women are cast in television programming. T F
16. Watching violence on television for long periods of time reduces one's sensitivity toward acts of violence in real-life situations. T F
17. Television tends to shape the lifestyles of children. T F
18. Some television viewing for children is desirable. Research shows that 96 percent of the homes in the U.S. have at least 1 television, and one would not want a child to feel socially deprived in his or her development. T F
19. Watching the news on commercial television is generally an educational experience for a child. T F
20. Children from lower socioeconomic groups are more influenced by television violence than other groups. T F

. . . .

The Marriage Game

by J'Anne Stuckey

Age: Adult

Setting: 6–8 married couples

Time: 60 minutes

Goal: To make participants more aware of the romance in marriage and more attuned to their own needs and their partner's needs

Leader Preparation: Adapted from the TV show *The Newlywed Game;* look over the list of possible questions; be prepared to have various participants read the Scriptures aloud at the end of the exercise

Scripture: Philippians 2:3; 1 Thessalonians 4:18; 2 Thessalonians 1:3; Hebrews 3:13

The Exercise:
  A. Select one couple to be the host of the game. They will interview each person and keep score during the game. A set of questions is listed below, but others can be developed for any theme, for example, finances, children, or vacation plans.
  B. Ask the men to leave the room and ask the women their set of questions. Then, call the men back in and ask them to respond to the same set of questions, but to give the answers they think their wives would give. To make it more fun, award points for matching answers and keep score.
  C. Now, turn it around. Ask the wives to leave and ask the men their set of questions. Call the wives back in and have them respond to the same questions the way they think their husbands would. Again, award points for matching answers.
  D. This could be played men against women or couples against each other, depending on how you keep score.

. . . .

Questions for the Romance Topic:

MEN
1. What does your wife appreciate about you the most?
2. The most romantic time we had was_____.
3. If money were no object and you could take your wife anywhere in the world, where would you take her?
4. If it were up to your wife, how often would you "go on a date"?
5. What do you appreciate most about your wife?

WOMEN
1. When did you first realize that you wanted to marry your husband?
2. Your husband's idea of a romantic date is _____.
3. If you really want to please your husband in an extra special way, you would _____.
4. The time you communicated best as a couple was _____.
5. Next to spending time with you, what is it that your husband enjoys doing?

Summary and Conclusion:

Conclude with a group discussion. Try to guide the discussion toward two purposes. First, allow each person to honestly state feelings and opinions about marriage expectations and gender roles in our society. Challenge stereotypes and use probing questions to encourage individuals to back up their ideas.

Secondly, have group members read the Scriptures aloud. As a group compare and contrast what Scripture says with what we encounter in our culture. Let the group bring up additional Scriptures that apply. Would anyone want to intentionally take a stand counter to the culture on certain items as a result of this game and discussion? How specifically might he or she live this out during the coming week? If the group is interested, brainstorm some ideas and make a mutual commitment.

Exercise Twenty-Six

Abstention Tension

by Armin Sommer

Age: Adult

Setting: Groups on planning retreats, board meetings, or training sessions (especially church leadership) up to about 30 participants (more than 30 may be cumbersome)

Time: 45–60 minutes

Goal: To give leaders a practical opportunity to grapple with conflicting authorities and opinions about Christian lifestyle choices in the local church

Leader Preparation: Have volunteers prepared to role-play the introductory drama; copies of Questions to Ponder (p. 237) to stimulate group discussion; Bibles and concordances available for reference

Scripture: Exodus 20:12; Ephesians 6:1; 1 Timothy 3; 5:1–2; Titus 2:1–6, 3:1–9; 1 Peter 5:1–5

The Exercise:
A. Leader reads aloud Exodus 20:12.
B. Role Play
   Hans Sommer is a born-again believer who has grown up in West Germany in a town that produces one of the great European wines. Hans recently immigrated to the United States and works for an importing firm. Desiring Christian fellowship, he applied for membership at the First Baptist Church of Garb, Colorado. At this moment, the board of deacons is interviewing Hans. They ask him to present his testimony, describe his vocation, and give an account of his Christian lifestyle. As they do so, the subject of the church covenant arises, which states in article XXII (3) (a): "We furthermore promise to abstain from the consumption or sale of any and all alcoholic beverages."

The chairman of the board mentions that all church members are required to sign the church covenant. The discussion continues, with both parties being visibly upset. (*Note:* The role play should be terminated before any decision to sign or not sign the covenant.)

C. Class Discussion

    1. Before discussion begins, pass out papers with the following questions and choices for individuals to ponder alone.

Questions to Ponder

a) What do you think of such a requirement as this one in the church covenant?

    _____ Seems reasonable. I would not mind signing such a statement.

    _____ Seems unreasonable but not a big issue. Not worth making a fuss over.

    _____ Seems unreasonable and a serious matter. I would no longer seek membership at this church and believe they should change their covenant.

    _____ Write out any other position here.

b) Scriptures I base my conclusions on include the following:

    2. Allow participants to share their opinions from the Questions to Ponder, perhaps concluding with a show of hands to support their decision.

    3. In fact, Hans did sign the covenant, but under protest. Why do you think Hans protested this requirement?

    4. Was Hans ethically correct in signing a covenant he sincerely felt was wrong? Why or why not?

    5. Five years later, under a new pastor and with Hans as chairman of the deacon board, the church removed from the covenant the clause prohibiting the consumption or sale of alcohol. Under what conditions do you think the church should change rules when people object? Can anyone cite a scriptural example? (Hint: Try the book of Acts.)

Summary and Conclusion:

What is the real, underlying issue here? Perhaps you will want to discuss the general principles of relationships between church members and the elders or deacons of the church. What would you have done in the specific situation described? What will you do in the future under such circumstances? What Scriptures come to mind that you think need to be applied to this sort of situation?

. . . .

Appendixes

• •

Summarizing the Stages of Intellectual Growth and Moral Development

God created the solar system and the galaxies, and we humans can explore their grandeur and marvel at His order and consistency. Just so, God has placed within humankind, His special creation, an order and consistency. We glimpse this marvelous order when we observe the way a child grows and develops into an adult. Truly an inner clock guides this entire miraculous process. Becoming familiar with God's order reduces frustration and makes our teaching more effective.

Listed in the bibliography at the end of this book are several excellent books that explain human growth in detail. But we also want to present here a brief overview of two areas of growth: (1) intellectual development, and (2) stages of moral development. It's important for Christian workers to understand both of these types of growth, because students (children and adults) need to have attained a certain level of intellectual development before they are able to deal with specific levels of moral choices.

Stages of Intellectual or Cognitive Development

Briefly, intellectual development has been divided into four stages by Piaget. The ages listed are approximate. During the first stage, from birth to approximately age two, most of the child's intellectual energy is focused on **sensorimotor** development. For example, children learn that their hands are connected to their arms and, by much practice, how to make them pick up and let go of the objects that their eyes are learning to focus on. This is a huge task in itself. Along with this, babies will be learning about *object constancy*—the reality that even if they can't see it anymore, an object will remain where they left it. This is why babies think playing "Peekaboo" is such a kick! On the other hand, when Mom does leave for a couple of hours, a toddler may become inconsolable, because "later" means nothing. Since toddlers have not developed enough to understand time, if Mom is gone now, as far as the toddler is concerned, she's gone "forever."

• •

The next stage of growth, the **pre-operational**, takes place from approximately age two to age seven. Kids at this time are learning language. Although they know lots of words, they take everything very literally, and it's a step for them to put together two different facts to come up with a third, different, conclusion. In other words, they are not often "logical" by adult standards, and the conclusions they do come up with often amuse adults. Harold's granddaughter, who is four years old, couldn't believe that he could be her grandfather because the grandfather lived in Wheaton. At this stage children learn *perceptual constancy*, that a piece of clay rolled into a long "snake," for example, is not any larger or smaller than when it's rolled into a ball.

Between ages seven to eleven, in the **concrete operations** stage, children grow in their ability to remember facts, to organize and classify facts, and to compare and contrast facts. They become able to see individual items as parts of a larger system. Now they understand time concepts like "before," "now," and "later." However, children at this age are not really able to deal with abstract ideas. For example, they will be unable to catch on to the humor of a pun.

This capacity for abstract thought arrives when they reach the final stage of intellectual or cognitive development, **formal operations,** which start at age eleven and continues on through adulthood. (Research reveals some normal individuals lack the capacity to grasp abstract math concepts—such as algebra—until the late teens or early twenties.) All the typical adolescent and adult "deep questions" about the meaning of life and complex moral conflicts require a capacity for abstract thinking. It is important to remember this distinction when dealing with grade-school children and to avoid the use of complex analogies or similes to express truth, because the children will not be able to grasp them as an adult would (although they may be able to parrot back the "correct" answer if drilled). The chart in appendix 8 (p. 251–52) gives further information about Piaget's stages.

Levels of Moral Development

Moral development refers to how people grow in their ability to resist temptation, to obey their conscience, and to decide what is right or wrong in a situation they have never encountered before.

One researcher, Lawrence Kohlberg, divides moral development into three levels. Then, each level is subdivided into two stages. So, while there are three levels of moral growth, there are six stages of moral growth. Unlike intellectual development, growth through the various levels of moral development is not inevitable. It is possible to be mature intellectually and immature morally if nothing has happened to stimulate your moral development.

On the other hand, each level of moral development demands a certain amount of cognitive development before it is possible to achieve it. For example, the toddler with no intellectual grasp of the concept of time cannot develop moral scruples about being tardy and inconveniencing others. But the intellectually mature adult, who grasps an abstract concept like time, may still be motivated to be prompt by a simple fear of punishment (Level One) rather than an unselfish desire to do what is best for everyone (Level Three).

What this means in practical terms for Christian education is that children and adults who are living below the level of moral development *could be* intellectually nudged to grow on to the next moral level. Often, feeling baffled and challenged by a moral conflict is what stimulates people to grow. All the exercises in this book are designed to take into account both types of growth— intellectual and moral. They are at the right intellectual development level for the average age listed on the heading. In addition they are planned to stimulate or reinforce the highest level of moral development that would match that age.

Level One of moral development, called the Preconventional Level, has two stages. In both stages the child's motivation is mostly from outside events. In Stage One, Punishment and Obedience (ages five to six) children determine right from wrong by whether or not they get punished. If they get away with something, they may conclude it's not wrong after all. At this stage children unquestioningly accept that what their parents say is right or wrong, because their parents are much bigger and more powerful than they are. With Stage Two of Level One, the Instrumental Relativist Stage (ages seven to ten), children are very interested in "fairness" as a way to get what they want. They can be motivated by the hope of a reward to do what is right. But they focus in on the reward much more than on doing right for its own sake.

Level Two is called the Conventional Level. Here conforming and meeting the expectations of one's family or peers and nation is the great motivator. In Stage Three, called Good Boy/Nice Girl (ages ten to twelve), good behavior is defined as being able to please others and earn their approval. In Stage Four, the Law and Order Stage (ages twelve to sixteen), the focus is on doing one's duty and respecting authority. Never mind a person's motivation, does the person follow the rules?

At this level the youth group may be the most powerful influence in developing current values. Boys at this stage tend to push away from their mothers' values and identify with their fathers' values. When the boy doesn't have a father, he is more apt to identify with a respected male authority figure in his life.

Jesus nudged the people of His day into a higher stage of moral growth when He challenged the status quo established by the Pharisees with His Sermon on the Mount. Jesus insisted that a person's "heart" (motivation) for doing right was just as important as the person's behavior.

The highest level of moral development, Level Three, is labeled the Autonomous or Principled Level. As Kohlberg defined it, this level moves beyond social conformity to grapple with what is truly just for all of society—not just my little group—and how to achieve a consensus among several competing interests to choose what's in the best interests of all.

Stage Five of Level Three is labeled Social-contract, Legalistic (early or middle twenties, if ever). A healthy democracy in which the majority rules without trampling on minority opinions is an example of this stage in action.

An individual may never reach Stage Six of Level Three and probably won't before age thirty. Abstract concepts, such as the Golden Rule, form the basis for moral judgments here, rather than concrete rules (for example, "You may walk only five cubits on the Sabbath"). By the time people reach this stage, they must be willing and able to stand alone for what they believe is right even if this requires going against the tide of popular opinion. Of course, if they belong to a church that holds the same set of values, they will find the church far more helpful to them in building a strong set of biblical values that are consistent with the church's belief system. It is just this sort of moral independence that we want to see in mature Christians (see Romans 12:2).

Appendix Two

Ten Value-Rich Areas

1. Money
2. Friendship
3. Love and sex
4. Religion and morals
5. Leisure
6. Politics
7. Work
8. Family
9. Maturity
10. Character traits

Appendix Three

Thirty Clarifying Responses

1. Is this something that you prize?
2. Are you glad about that?
3. How did you feel when that happened?
4. Did you consider any alternatives?
5. Have you felt this way for a long time?
6. Was that something that you yourself selected or chose?
7. Did you *have* to choose that? Was it a free choice?
8. Do you *do* anything about that idea?
9. Can you give me some examples of that idea?
10. What do you mean by *(example)*, can you define that word?
11. Where would that idea lead? What would be its consequences?
12. Would you really *do* that or are you just talking?
13. Are you saying that . . . (repeat the statement)?
14. Did you say that . . . (repeat in some distorted way)?
15. Have you thought much about that notion?
16. What are some good things about that notion?
17. What do we have to assume for things to work out that way?
18. Is what you express consistent with . . . (note something else the person said or did that may point to an inconsistency)?
19. What other possibilities are there?
20. Is that a personal preference or do you think most people should believe that?
21. How can I help you do something about your idea?
22. Is there a purpose back of this activity?
23. Is that very important to you?
24. Do you do this often?
25. Would you like to tell others about your idea?
26. Do you have any reasons for saying (or doing) that?
27. Would you do the same thing over again?
28. How do you know it's right?
29. Do you value that?
30. Do you think people will always believe that?

Twenty-One Clarifying Strategies

1. The clarifying response (see appendix 5)
2. The value sheet
3. The value-clarifying discussion
4. Role playing
5. The contrived incident
6. Zig-zag lessons
7. Devil's advocate
8. Value continuum
9. Thought sheets
10. Weekly reaction sheets
11. Open-ended questions
12. Coded student papers
13. Time diaries
14. Autobiographical questionnaires
15. Public interviews
16. Decision-making interviews
17. Voting
18. Five-minute quotes without comment
19. Student reports
20. Action projects
21. An approach to self-conception

Clarifying Responses Suggested by the Seven Valuing Processes

1. Choosing Freely
   a) Where do you suppose you first got that idea?
   b) How long have you felt that way?
   c) What would people say if you weren't to do what you say you must do?
   d) Are you getting help from anyone? Do you need more help? Can I help?
   e) Are you the only one in your crowd who feels that way?
   f) What do your parents want you to be/do?
   g) Is there any rebellion in your choice?
   h) How many years will you give to it? What will you do if you're not good enough?
   i) Do you think the idea of having thousands of people cheering when you come out on the field has anything to do with your choice?
2. Choosing from Alternatives
   a) What else did you consider before you picked this?
   b) How long did you look around before you decided?
   c) Was it a hard decision? What went into the final decision? Who helped? Do you need any further help?
   d) Did you consider another possible alternative?
   e) Are there some reasons behind your choice?
   f) What choices did you reject before you settled on your present idea or action?
   g) What's really good about this choice that makes it stand out from the other possibilities?

3. Choosing Thoughtfully and Reflectively
   a) What would be the consequences of each alternative available?
   b) Have you thought about this very much? How did your thinking go?
   c) Is this what I understand you to say . . . (interpret the statement)?
   d) Are you implying that . . . (distort the statement to see if he or she is clear enough to correct the distortion)?
   e) What assumptions are involved in your choice? Let's examine them.
   f) Define the terms you use. Give me an example of the kind of job you can get without a high school diploma.
   g) Now if you do this, what will happen to that . . . ?
   h) Is what you say consistent with what you said earlier?
   i) Just what is good about this choice?
   j) Where will this choice lead?
   k) For whom are you doing this?
   l) With these other choices, rank them in order of significance.
   m) What will you have to do? What are your first steps? Second steps?
   n) Whom else did you talk to?
   o) Have you really weighed it fully?
4. Prizing and Cherishing
   a) Are you glad you feel that way?
   b) How long have you wanted it?
   c) What good is it? What purpose does it serve? Why is it important to you?
   d) Should everyone do it our way?
   e) Is it something you really prize?
   f) In what way would life be different without it?
5. Affirming
   a) Would you tell the class the way you feel some time?
   b) Would you be willing to sign a petition supporting that idea?
   c) Are you saying that you believe . . . (repeat the idea)?
   d) You don't mean to say you believe . . . (repeat the idea)?
   e) Should a person who believes the way you do speak out?
   f) Do people know that you believe that way or that you do that thing?
   g) Are you willing to stand up and be counted for that?
6. Acting upon Your Choices
   a) I hear what you are for; now, is there anything you can do about it? Can I help?
   b) What are your first steps, second steps, etc.?
   c) Are you willing to put some of your money behind this idea?
   d) Have you examined the consequences behind this idea?
   e) Are there any organizations set up for the same purpose? Will you join?
   f) Have you done much reading on the topic? Who has influenced you?
      (1) Have you made any plans to do more than you have already done?

(2) Would you want other people to know you feel this way? What if they disagree with you?

(3) Where will this lead you? How far are you willing to go?

(4) How has it already affected your life? How will it affect it in the future?

7. Repeating
   a) Have you felt this way for some time?
   b) Have you done anything already? Do you do this often?
   c) What are your plans for doing more of it?
   d) Should you get other people interested and involved?
   e) Has it been worth time and money?
   f) Are there some other things you can do that are like it?
   g) How long do you think you will continue?
   h) What did you *not* do when you went to do that? Was that OK?
   i) How did you decide which had priority?
   j) Did you run into any difficulty?
   k) Will you do it again?

Goals of Values Education

by Dr. Harold J. Westing

1. To lead a person to a born-again state in Christ so that he or she will have the spiritual dynamic (power) to perceive God's mind or point of view on ethical and moral issues and decisions (Phil. 1:6).
2. To help people to know the moral law of God so they will be conversant with it and know when and how to apply it. They should, as well, be able to see God's pragmatics in that law (Ps. 119:97ff.). Then they should be committed to that course of action publicly on a continuous basis with a knowledge of the rationale behind that course of action (Deut. 6:1–2).
3. To help people become autonomous so they can make informed judgments of their own even if it is contrary to the norms of their peers and society (Rom. 12:1–2).
4. To foster within them the desire to gain sufficient data so that when they are faced with alternative values they will make autonomously a wise decision.
5. To teach them a sufficient amount of moral language and the logic behind that language so they can become prescriptive with that information, both for themselves and others.
6. To develop a sensitivity and insight into one's own and other's needs, feelings, and interests so that moral judgment is for the good of the group, not just for the individual. One will have to be in communication with a wide range of people to know those needs.
7. Ultimately, to help people become facilitators in causing others also to make principled decisions at each stage of their moral development. This may necessitate changing existing rules among their peer groups.
8. To be able to equip parents and teachers to foster a rational appraisal of proper values as they converse with children so they will make their own autonomous rational decisions about morality.

Guidelines for Making Values Decisions

by Dr. Harold J. Westing

A. Scriptural guidelines
  1. Seek the Bible for principles that apply to this situation.
  2. Be willing to let Scripture influence my decision over against what my peers or society may say.
  3. Seek for and be willing to be guided by every portion of Scripture even when it may cost me greatly to follow its guidelines.
  4. When an issue is unclear, seek to do as I believe Christ would in this situation.
B. Personal guidelines
  1. Be willing to stand alone for a decision even when it may cost me a great deal of time or money.
  2. Be sure to face the issues at stake without letting just my emotions rule my choice.
  3. Be willing to change my mind when I am wrong, even if it means being embarrassed on an issue.
  4. Be willing to take a decisioned action:
     • not because others will think well of me.
     • not because I want to please others.
     • not because it satisfies my needs.
     • not because I'm afraid I will get caught.
     • BUT because I have proved it is the right answer.
C. Issue guidelines
  1. Be certain to look at all the facts in the issue, not just the ones that seem to affirm my side of the case.
  2. Be consistent in the decision. I will seek to use all the principles in this case as I would in any similar situation.
  3. Be willing to project myself into the future and consider the long-range consequences rather than just the immediate situation.

D. Action guidelines
   1. Be certain to show that this is a value to me by acting upon my decision and not just saying I believe it is my value.
   2. Be willing to affirm my decision by affirming its rightness in repeatedly doing the same.
   3. Be certain to take responsibility in helping to carry out my plan.

Teaching of Religious Concepts

An Outline of Piaget's Stages of Intellectual Development

Stage	Approximate Ages	Some Characteristic Cognitive Developments
Pre-Operational	2–7 years	*Object constancy*. Once language and internal representation of the world begin to develop, mental as well as physical objects acquire permanence. Children realize an object continues to exist even when they do not perceive it. *Little capacity* to grasp time, distance, and numbers. Thinking has *little flexibility* and usually proceeds step-by-step in only one direction. Thinking is transductive. They cannot group ideas together and draw a central principle. Children's thoughts are characterized by *syncretism*. Syncretistic thinking links items and events together that do not belong together. Thought is dominated by *centering*. This is a tendency to focus attention

on one characteristic or feature of an idea or experience and fail to see other important aspects.

Thinking is *"irreversible."* Children can follow a sequence of operations but cannot trace a sequence back to the original starting point.

Children cannot assimilate other points of view. *Perceptions dominate* their thinking. They are greatly influenced by what they see, hear, or otherwise experience at a given moment.

Concrete Operations 7–11 years

Children becomes less egocentric in their thinking. The child understands and uses certain principles or relationships between things and ideas. This type of thinking is still rooted to events and objects that are concrete (visual experience and data apprehended through sensory activity). Thinking is reversible. Thus, in certain learning situations children can check on their conclusions.

The child begins to master conservation abilities. Substance, weight, length, area, volume, and number remain the same (are conserved) even when changes are made in arrangements and positions.

Formal   11 years
Operations   and after

Individuals can think in terms of abstract symbols instead of having to base their thoughts on concrete things and events. Individuals can entertain concepts with which they have had no real experience—such as the notion of infinity.

Individuals are free to move in their thoughts and are flexible. They are not stuck with their perceptions or their conclusions. Individuals can think about their own thinking.

Building Biblical Values

Selected Bibliography

Clouse, Bonnidell. *Teaching for Moral Growth*. Wheaton, Ill.: Victor Books/ SP Publications, 1993.

Duska, Ronald, and Mariellen Whelan. *Moral Development*. New York: Paulist Press, 1975.

Fowler, James. *Becoming Adult, Becoming Christian*. New York: Harper & Row, 1984.

Garrett, Wilma. *Kids Will Listen to You If . . .* Wheaton, Ill.: Leader Enrichment, Inc., 1976.

Hennessy, Thomas C. *Values and Moral Development*. New York: Paulist Press, 1976.

Krebs, Richard. *How to Bring Up a Good Child*. Minneapolis: Augsburg Publishing House, 1980.

Larson, Jim. *Rights, Wrongs, and In-Betweens*. Minneapolis: Augsburg Publishing House, 1984.

Raths, Louis E., Merrill Harmin, and Sidney B. Simon. *Values and Teaching*. Columbus, Ohio: Charles E. Merrill Publishing Co., 1966.

Simon, Sidney B., Leland W. Howe, and Howard Kirschenbaum. *Values Clarification*. New York: Hart Publishing Co., 1972.

Simpson, Bert K. *Becoming Aware of Values*. San Diego: Pennent Press, 1973.

Stonehouse, Catherine M. *Patterns in Moral Development*. Waco, Tex.: Word Incorporated, 1980.

Ward, Ted. *Values Begin at Home*. Wheaton, Ill.: Victor Books/SP Publications, 1989.

Winn, Marie. *The Plug-In Drug*. New York: Bantam Books, 1980.

Wolterstorff, Nicholas. *Educating for Responsible Action*. Grand Rapids: Wm. B. Eerdmans Publishing Co., 1980.

Zuck, Roy B., and Gene Getz. *Christian Youth: An In-Depth Study*. Chicago: Moody Press, 1968.

About the Authors

Penny Thome has a B.S. in Nursing, an A.A. in Technical Writing and Editing, and several years of experience in writing and editing for national distribution, including video scripts and a text for registered nurses.

She has worked as a psychiatric nurse with children with behavioral disorders, as an academic tutor with children with learning difficulties, and as a volunteer in Sunday school and vacation Bible school. Also, she helped to develop, train staff, and teach curriculum for a children's divorce recovery series; she has served as Staff Trainer and Dean of Women with a Christian camp for neglected, abandoned, and abused children.

Dr. Harold J. Westing, a graduate of Moody Bible Institute, Grace College, and Western Seminary, has served as a state and national director of Christian Education for the Conservative Baptist Association of America. During nineteen years at Denver Seminary, he was Dean of Students and Professor of Christian Education and Pastoral Ministries. He introduced a course on values education while teaching at the seminary. He and his wife, Betty, have three children and five grandchildren. He is a recognized authority on church growth and Christian education. His books include *Evaluate and Grow, I'd Love to Tell the World, Super Superintendent, Church Staff Handbook,* and *Create and Celebrate Your Church's Uniqueness.*